AMERICAN APOSTASY

We are living in an era when "a famine of the hearing of the Lord" (Amos 8:11, 12) is widespread. Likewise, our nations foundations and history are being revised and undermined to accommodate a godless agenda. Pastor Todd Gould has assembled chapters that are both historically accurate and scripturally relevant to the end that we who have trusted Christ would remember the grace and ancient formulas that lead to God's blessing.

Pastor Dean Stewart

Todd R. Gould expertly connects our nation's spiritual condition with the temporal position. *American Apostasy* provides critical insight for times like this and the days ahead. This book provides a sober and provocative case that demands a verdict.

Nathan B. Franklin, Esq.

Some readers will nod in agreement. Some readers will shake their heads in disbelief. All readers will be challenged to think. Thus, I heartily endorse Todd's book.

Rev. Jack Hager
Ministry Liaison
Truth Impact

AMERICAN APOSTASY

By

TODD R. GOULD

Book Cover: "The Lost Sheep" by Alfred M. Soord from the collections of the University of Southern California and the California Historical Society. Used by permission.

Cover Design: Mark T. Anderson

All scripture references are taken from the New American Standard Bible 1995 (NASB 1995) unless otherwise noted.

ISBN 978-0-9600115-4-4 (Paperback)
978-0-9600115-5-1 (Digital)

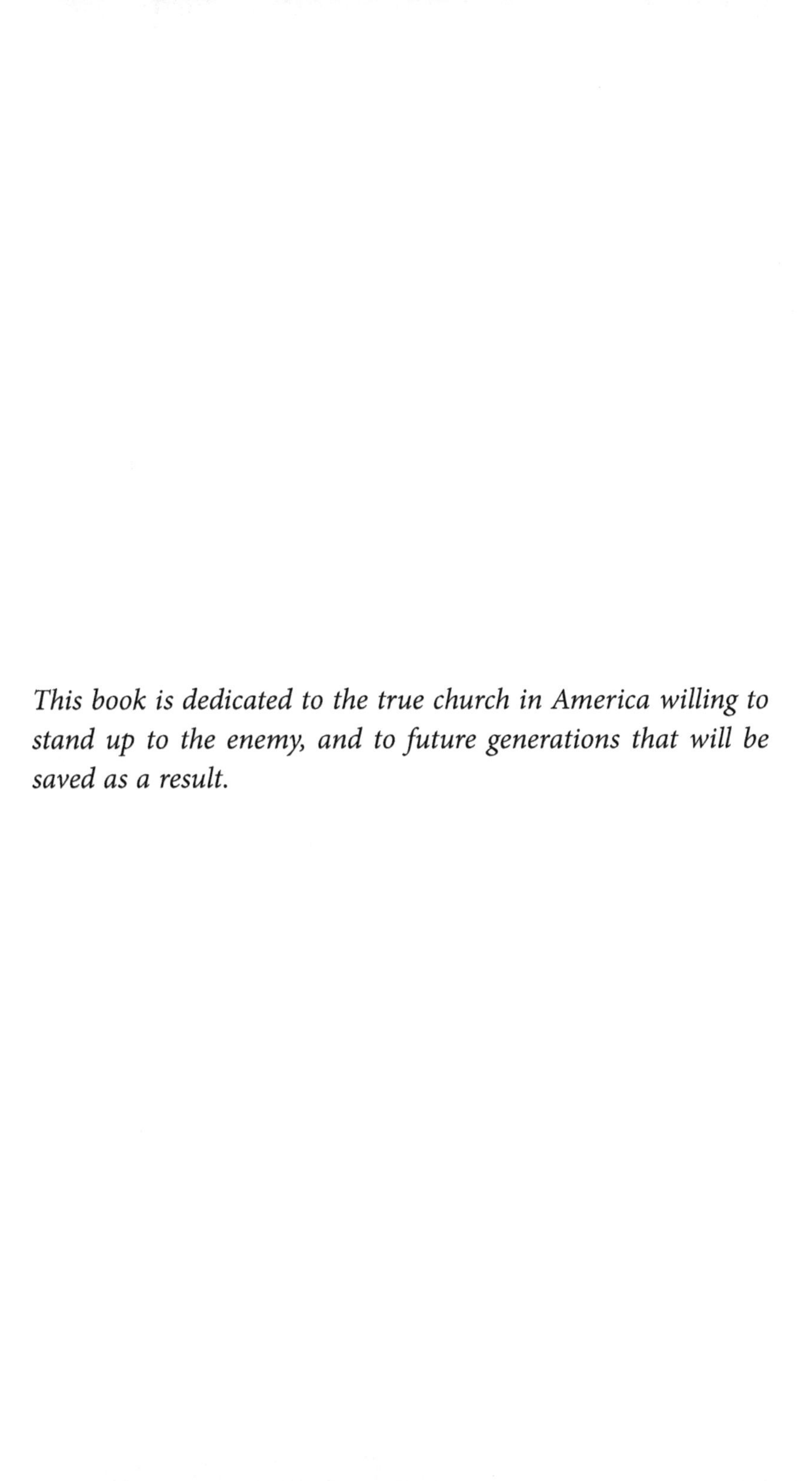

This book is dedicated to the true church in America willing to stand up to the enemy, and to future generations that will be saved as a result.

Table of Contents

Introduction

It's been said, judgment isn't coming to America, judgment is already here! Observing the current chaotic conditions in the U.S., what other conclusion can be made? Why judgment? The same reason as always – spiritual apostasy. My goal in writing this book is to bring Christian citizens to an awareness of, not just the symptoms of apostasy, but its cause, and ultimately its cure.

In the opening chapters, I lay out America's spiritual foundations. Then, finding biblical parallels with God's chosen Israel, application is made to Christian America. God's call, God's blessings, and God's chastisement for spiritual failure are all seen in His dealings with the ancient nation, an object lesson for America today.

To the unenlightened eye, our problems appear to be material and physical. But it takes a spiritual eye to see beyond the horizontal and into the vertical, the spiritual dimension where true answers are found. And, as the issue of apostasy (falling away) is spiritual in nature, spiritual tools/weapons must be employed for its remedy. These are revealed at the conclusion of this writing in hopes that the church will once again take them up and defeat the enemy that has brought us to this place.

May we have that "victory in Jesus!"

Blessings,
TRG

CHAPTER 1

America's Foundation

The first settlers who came from England landed on the North American continent for the express purpose of propagating the faith of Christ. This truth is clearly seen in our earliest historical documents available today.

The first permanent English colony was founded at Jamestown, Virginia (named after King James I) on May 13th, 1607. Its royal charter read:

> We, greatly commending, and graciously accepting of, their desires for the furtherance of so noble a work, which may by the providence of Almighty God, hereafter tend to the glory of his divine Majesty, in propagating the Christian religion to such people, as yet live in darkness and miserable ignorance of the true knowledge and worship of God, and may in time bring the infidels and savages, living in those parts, to human civility, and to a quiet and settled government; Do, by these our letters pattents, graciously accept of, and agree to, their humble and well intended desires.[1]

The original charter showed far more interest in commerce than it did conversion. However, later settlers reinforced the missionary effort. Despite a series of hardships and setbacks, leaders like John Rolfe believed there was a Christian purpose for Jamestown and he sought to "advance the honor of God, and to propagate his gospel." He believed there was "no small hope by piety, clemency, courtesy and civil demeanor to convert and bring to the knowledge and true worship of Jesus Christ 1000s of poor wretched and misbelieving people: on whose faces a good Christian cannot look, without sorrow, pity and commiseration, seeing they bear the image of our heavenly Creator, and we and they come from one and the same mold…"[2]

Hardships, sufferings, difficulties, and disappointments continued in the Virginia settlements throughout the early years. Alexander Whitaker, minister at Henrics, Virginia, in 1612 reminded the people that their problems were indicative of the great spiritual struggle in the new land.[3]

On November 11th, 1620, thirteen years later, another group of religious separatists we know as the "Pilgrims," landed at Cape Cod. Before setting foot on dry land, the weary, storm tossed group recognized the importance of establishing a covenant of purpose and governance, thus drafting what is known as *The Mayflower Compact.* It reads:

> In the name of God, Amen. We, whose names are underwritten, the Loyal Subjects of our dread Sovereign Lord, King James, by the grace of God, of England, France, and Ireland, King, Defender of the Faith,…

> Having undertaken for the glory of God, and advancement of the Christian Faith, and the Honour of our King and Country, a voyage to plant the first colony in the northern parts of Virginia; do by these presents, solemnly and mutually in the Presence of God and one another, covenant and combine ourselves together into a Civil Body Politic, for our better Ordering and Preservation, and Furtherance of the Ends, aforesaid; And by virtue hereof to enact, constitute, and frame such just and equal Laws, Ordinances, Acts, Constitutions, and Offices, from time to time, as shall be thought most meet and convenient for the general good of the Colony; unto which we promise all due submission and obedience.
>
> In Witness whereof we have hereunto subscribed our names at Cape Cod the eleventh of November, in the reign of our Sovereign Lord, King James of England, France, and Ireland, the eighteenth, and of Scotland the fifty-fourth, Anno Domini, 1620.

This vital declaration was not only a statement of Christian purpose, but also the foundation of self-government under God, ultimately influencing our Declaration of Independence and U.S. Constitution a century and a half later. But in another ten years, an even more devout group would establish itself in the Massachusetts Bay Colony.

Though the Pilgrims wanted to separate themselves from the Church of England, this group of Anglicans sought to purify it. The Puritans endeavored to build a colony in the

New World that would reflect strong biblical values and Calvinist theology. A charter granted by King Charles established a new trading organization known as the Massachusetts Bay Company which would transfer to the Massachusetts Bay Colony. John Winthrop was elected governor.

Before the first group of 400 Puritans set sail for the New World, Winthrop gave a speech (sermon) that detailed their godly mission. His message titled *A Model of Christian Charity* (also know as *A City on a Hill*) was a beautiful exposition of Christian hope and burgeoning opportunity. Here is a portion of that sermon:

> Thus stands the cause between God and us. We are entered into covenant with Him for this work. We have taken out a commission. The Lord hath given us leave to draw our own articles. We have professed to enterprise these and those accounts, upon these and those ends. We have hereupon besought Him of favor and blessing. Now if the Lord shall please to hear us, and bring us in peace to the place we desire, then hath He ratified this covenant and sealed our commission, and will expect a strict performance of the articles contained in it; but if we shall neglect the observation of these articles which are the ends we have propounded, and, dissembling with our God, shall fail to embrace this present world and prosecute our carnal intentions, seeking great things for ourselves and our posterity, the Lord will surely break out in wrath against us, and

be revenged of such a people, and make us know the price of the breach of such a covenant.

Now the only way to avoid this shipwreck, and to provide for our posterity is to follow the counsel of Micah, to do justly, to love mercy, to walk humbly with our God. For this end, we must be knit together, in this work, as one man. We must entertain each other in brotherly affection. We must be willing to abridge ourselves of our superfluities, for the supply of others' necessities. We must uphold a familiar commerce together in all meekness, gentleness, patience and liberality. We must delight in each other; make others' conditions our own, rejoice together, mourn together, labor and suffer together, always having before our eyes our commission and community in the work, as members of the same body. So shall we keep the unity of the Spirit in the bond of peace. The Lord will be our God, and delight to dwell among us, as His own people, and will command a blessing upon us in all our ways, so that we will see much more of His wisdom, power, goodness and truth, than formerly we have been acquainted with. We shall find that the God of Israel is among us, when ten of us shall be able to resist a thousand of our enemies; when He shall make us a praise and glory that men shall say of succeeding plantations, "may the Lord make it like that of New England." *For we must consider that we shall be as a city upon a hill. The eyes of all people are upon us. So that if we shall deal falsely with our God in this work we have undertaken, and so cause Him to withdraw His present help from us, we shall be made a story and a by-word through the world.* We shall open the mouths of enemies to speak evil of the ways of God, and all professors for God's sake. We shall shame the faces of many of God's worthy servants, and cause their prayers to be turned into curses upon us till we be consumed out of the good land whither we are going.

And to shut this discourse with the exhortation of Moses, that faithful servant of the Lord, in his last farewell to Israel, Deut. 30. "Beloved, there is now set before us life and death, good and evil," in that we are commanded this day to love the Lord our God, and to love one another, to walk in His ways and to keep his Commandments and his ordinance and his laws, and the articles of our Covenant with Him, that we may live and be multiplied, and that the Lord our God may bless us in the land whither we go to possess it. *But if our hearts shall turn away, so that we will not obey, but shall be seduced, and worship other Gods, our pleasure and profits, and serve them; it is propounded unto us this day, we shall surely perish out of the good land whither we pass over this vast sea to possess it.*

Therefore let us choose life,
that we and our seed may live,
by obeying His voice and cleaving to Him,
for He is our life and our prosperity.[4]

President Ronald Reagan, ever the optimist, quoted the "Shining City on a Hill" portion of Winthrop's message in his 1989 farewell address to the nation. There Reagan gave John Winthrop credit for his wonderful vision of America's potential future, a vision reinvigorated during his eight-year presidency. Of course, John Winthrop quoted Matthew 5:14-16, Christ's Sermon on the Mount, so Reagan, through Winthrop, also quoted Christ. We see, from this interaction, how great men are connected to one another. Which reminds me of a maxim oft quoted at the Bible Institute I attended: "Fellowship with great minds, and you, in turn, will become great." The exhortation was to read, study, and meditate upon the works of other great historical figures in order to gain and apply the wisdom and knowledge they had already gleaned from life and learning. But isn't that what true education is supposed to be? Aren't students to learn and grow and benefit from the lessons their predecessors have already accumulated?

Another adage I heard was: "Quote others or you will never be quoted." Well, here I am, quoting a professor, who quoted someone else, and Ronald Reagan, who quoted John Winthrop, who quoted Jesus Christ, who quoted the Heavenly Father (John 8:26-28). It's amazing how truth, wisdom, and knowledge are traced back to the One who is Truth, Wisdom, and Knowledge personified, isn't it? And we are blessed with the same when we get connected to Him.

The point of this chapter is to demonstrate the connection Americans have to their past; to show how our godly forefathers laid a foundation of Christian faith in a new land and incorporated it into their lives, their commerce, and especially their government. The secularly indoctrinated will protest and say, "The Constitution declares there must be a separation between church and state in the establishment clause." These secularists take Thomas Jefferson's words in a letter (not the Constitution) to the Danbury Baptist Association "a wall of separation between church and state" to mean there should be no connection at all between government and church. However, all colonial constitutions included specific statements regarding incorporation of the Christian faith into government – emphasis on *Christian* faith. The term "religion" as used by the founders always meant Christianity. They never thought Americans would ever consider any other. The issue the Danbury Baptists had was with the Calvinist government of Connecticut that infringed upon their own religious liberty as provided for in the First Amendment.

The early Puritans of Massachusetts believed in the separation of church and state, but not a separation of the state from God, which is advocated today. Unfortunately, Winthrop's vision of "a shining city on a hill" faded away with his generation as non-Puritans and settlers with less honorable intentions moved into the colony. Though the Puritan "errand to the wilderness" went largely unrealized, their concept of personal freedom and self-government, outlined in the Massachusetts Body of Liberties, and other places, greatly influenced the form of our soon to follow U.S. Constitution and Bill of Rights. This stands in contrast to the anti-American historical revisionists who intentionally contradict solidly documented American history.

The 1619 Project

The 1619 Project is one of the latest propaganda tropes foisted upon the U.S. public by those who would "fundamentally change America." Nikole Hannah Jones unabashedly declared slavery was the true founding of our nation in a collection of New York Times articles which eventually became a book. The "project" was begun on the supposed 400th anniversary of the arrival of the first slaves on the continent in Virginia. That assumption, like many others in the project, was roundly discredited by true historians, both liberal and conservative. Records of slavery go back as far as Columbus, and African slaves are known to have accompanied the Spanish as early as the 1500s. Of course, the woke anti-American/anti-Christian agenda is woven throughout and cynically labels crucial events, like the American Revolution, the American Civil War, and individuals like Abraham Lincoln and our Founders as "white supremacy."

Even though the 1619 Project lacked true scholarship and was racist to the core, much of its teaching found its way into our public school curriculum. To counter this anti-patriotic assault, President Trump appointed the 1776 Commission which exposed the 1619 Project for the fraud that it was. Of course, the Commission's January 2021 report was immediately attacked by liberal critics and the commission was terminated by Joe Biden two days later.

Unbelievably, Nikole Hannah-Jones was awarded a Pulitzer Prize in 2020 for this jaundiced falsification of American history. To declare African slavery and systematic racism the true foundation of America is foolish at best and intentionally seditious at worst. Surely, our foundation did have its faults, slavery being one, but the Pilgrims and the Puritans did not initially begin with it. The institution of slavery did not exist in the early days of New England but was legalized much later. However, by the time of the composition of the Declaration of Independence, men like John Adams, James Otis, Thomas Payne, Patrick Henry, Benjamin Franklin and many others stood in opposition to it. Certainly, slavery was a moral dilemma for most of those who signed a Declaration that read: "We hold these truths to be self-evident, that all men are created equal, that they are endowed by their Creator with certain unalienable rights, that among these are Life, Liberty and the pursuit of Happiness."

Conviction and conflict continued to dog the nation until this nagging moral and political problem was finally solved by a bloody Civil War. 360 thousand Union, and 260 thousand Confederate deaths made the payment on the debt of slavery in the U.S. Recent studies show those figures being much higher. This does not take into account the ghastly wounds and crippling disease that affected another half million servicemen on both sides, or the complete destruction of property in the South. Yes, the debt of slavery in America has long been paid. But at this very hour there is a movement to pay "reparations," so-called, to black citizens whose distant ancestors may, or may not, have been slaves – paid by people who were never slave owners. Somehow, injustice done to one group equates to justice for another.

Sadly, the wounds of racism that had been almost healed by the 21st century were intentionally reopened as one of the transformational tools of the Obama administration. As a result, we find ourselves now dealing with an artificially manufactured problem on which tax dollars are wasted. It reminds me of the illustration of the black ants and red ants put into a jar, living in relative peace, until someone shakes the jar.

It has always fascinated me that New Testament scripture never makes much of the slavery issue. Certainly, it was a major theme in the Old Testament, especially with regards to Israel's bondage in Egypt and their subsequent miraculous liberation by Jehovah. But at the time of the New Testament writings, biblical authors did not dwell on an institution in which 65% of the Roman Empire found itself. During Christ's earthly ministry, we never hear Him call for a slave rebellion, though He declared His mission was "to proclaim liberty to the captives, and freedom to prisoners" (Isaiah 61:1). Interestingly, Paul and the other inspired writers proudly claimed to be *bond servants*, i.e., *slaves* to the Lord Jesus Christ. In the Apostle Paul's charge to Pastor Timothy, he declared: "Let all who are under the yoke as slaves regard their own masters as worthy of all honor so that the name of God and our doctrine may not be spoken against. And let those who have believers as their masters not be disrespectful to them because they are brethren, but let them serve them all the more, because those who partake of the benefit are believers and beloved. Teach and preach these principles" (1st Timothy 6:1, 2). No rebellion, no reparations.

> Philemon 1:15, 16: "For perhaps it was for this reason that he was separated from you for a while, that you would have him back forever, no longer as a slave, but more than a slave, a beloved brother, especially to me, but how much more to you, both in the flesh and in the Lord." No retribution, no reparations.

> Galatians 3:2: "There is neither Jew nor Greek, there is neither slave nor free, there is neither male nor female; for you are all one in Christ Jesus." "If the Son sets you free, you really will be free" (John 8:36). Of course, it's not freedom the reparationists are seeking, but finances.

True freedom has its foundation in God's Word, and obedience to it. Our Founders understood this. After a century of blessing and prosperity, the vision of the "city on a hill" seen by Winthrop, Bradford and the first colonials was exchanged for a vision of complacency and comfort. The ardor and faith of our Puritan and Pilgrim forefathers settled into a spiritual malaise. Rationalism of the European Enlightenment had spread to the educated in America and common folks became preoccupied with all that the New World had to offer. However, certain godly clergymen like Theodore Frelinghuysen and Gilbert Tennant became alarmed at the spiritual dearth gripping the colonies and called their congregations to earnest prayer. First, the hearts of their own people changed, and then the youth began to go out to their own "Jerusalem,

Judea, Samaria and the remotest part of the earth" (Acts 1:8). A movement of the Holy Spirit was begun.

In 1741 the words of Jonathan Edwards, considered the father of the Great Awakening, pierced the hearts of his Northampton congregation. On July 8th of that year, Edwards delivered his famous message *Sinners in the Hands of an Angry God* in Enfield, Connecticut. Tales of people begging Edwards to stop when they felt the fires of hell consuming them, and fingernail prints dug into wooden pews as congregants grasped desperately to keep from slipping into the abyss, are told of that day. As his audience wailed and cried out, the pastor asked them to regain their composure so he could finish the sermon. From these seeds of revival a Great Awakening flourished and spread its canopy over the American colonies.

Other great men had a hand in God's wonderful work as well. John and Charles Wesley began drawing crowds along with their friend, George Whitefield, an Anglican evangelist who traveled throughout Britain and America. Whitefield, greatly gifted of the Lord for preaching, drew huge numbers with his resonant voice and Holy Spirit empowered messages. Kept from using available church facilities by jealous local pastors, Whitefield pioneered the open-air meeting where thousands came to faith. A very real spiritual transformation of the colonies and England continued under his ministry.

Benjamin Franklin became a close friend and a publisher of Whitefield's writings. He admired the evangelist for his great gifts and marveled at the effects his words had upon the listeners. After one outdoor meeting, Franklin measured the field where the people had gathered, estimating there was approximately 50,000 in attendance – and everyone was able to hear. An amazing feat, considering there was no public address system of any kind!

George Whitefield succeeded in unifying other revival movements that brought cohesion to the First Great Awakening. As a true unifier, the preacher was able to break down denominational barriers typified in a message he liked to preach:

> Father Abraham, who have you in heaven? Any Episcopalians? No! Any Presbyterians? No! Any independents or Methodists? No! No! No! Whom have you there then, Father Abraham?
>
> We don't know those names here! All who are here are Christians – believers in Christ, men who have overcome by the blood of the Lamb and the Word of His testimony.
>
> Oh, is that the case? Then God help me, and God help us all, to forget having names and to become Christians in deed and in truth![5]

The first spiritual awakening in America likely would not have happened if the original colonists did not bring with them a foundation of Christian faith. After all, *revival*, by definition, is bringing something back to life that was almost dead. It was God's will that His Spirit breathe new life into a dying church. This reinvigoration of Christianity upon the continent had a positive impact on the formation of what would become a new nation. The principles of God's Word have been copied into our founding documents as well as inscribed upon the edifices of Washington D.C., and most government buildings across the Republic. God blessed America as a result for He honors those who honor Him.

In 1st Samuel, Eli, the priest and judge of Israel, had become complacent in his ministry. He allowed his sons to abuse the sacrifice of the Lord and to commit adultery with the women who served at the tent of meeting. The Lord sent Eli a strong rebuke: "Why do you kick at My sacrifice and at My offering which I have commanded in My dwelling, and honor your sons above Me, by making yourselves fat with the choicest of every offering of My people Israel? Therefore the Lord God of Israel declares, 'I did indeed say that your house and the house of your father should walk before Me forever'; but now the Lord declares, 'Far be it from Me – for those who honor Me I will honor, and those who despise Me will be lightly esteemed'" (1st Samuel 2:29, 30). Soon, the Lord destroyed Eli's sons and, in judgment, blotted out his entire family line.

Today, the God of heaven who was once honored in America is no longer. Despite the abundance of material blessing and great liberty and protection He has afforded us, we, like ancient Israel, have turned our backs on Him. We have come to a place of disbelief and disdain for a Heavenly Father who has demonstrated amazing love and patience toward us. But as the Psalmist lamented: "If the foundations are destroyed, what can the righteous do?" (Psalm 11:3).

The foundations of our Christian past are being demolished by godless secularism now morphing into Marxist communism. The theological term that describes the U.S. is *apos-*

tate. Apostasy means turning away from the Christian position once held. We marvel at the insanity around us today and wonder "Why?" But the problem is not material, economic, or political. The problem is spiritual. Indeed, the cosmic struggle of good versus evil that has raged for aeons is now culminating in this generation on this planet. If the foundations are being destroyed, what the righteous *can* do is what we will take up in the next chapters.

CHAPTER 2

National Apostasy

There is a good chance most people don't know what the term *apostasy* means, though they may be guilty of it. Generally, *apostasy* (APOSTASIA in the Greek) means turning away from a former position. More specifically, apostasy pertains to those who have abandoned their faith in God and the Lord Jesus Christ – turning from light, returning to darkness. We could say apostasy is the opposite of conversion. Various types of turning away are seen throughout scripture, beginning with what I would consider the original apostate, Lucifer.

God's creation was perfect in every way. Lucifer, Star of the Morning, was also perfect and the most beautiful of the angelic host. We have two Old Testament scriptures that tell us about his fall in pre-history, Ezekiel 28 and Isaiah 14.

In Ezekiel's writing, God initially condemned the King of Tyre for his pride and arrogance. His island throne is recognized by the prophet, yet his ignoble end is also described in the first verses of Ezekiel 28. The language then changes in verses eleven through nineteen where the prophet speaks of an angelic being, a cherub, whose prideful attitude is very similar to that of the King of Tyre. Ezekiel 28:11-19:

11 Again the word of the Lord came to me saying,
12 "Son of man, take up a lamentation over the King
of Tyre, and say to him, 'Thus says the Lord God,
"You had the seal of perfection, full of wisdom and
perfect in beauty."
13 "You were in Eden, the garden of God; Every
precious stone was your covering: The ruby, the
topaz, and the diamond; The beryl, the onyx, and
the jasper; The lapis lazuli, the turquoise, and the
emerald; And the gold, the workmanship of your
settings and sockets, Was in you. On the day you
were created They were prepared.
14 "You were the anointed cherub who covers, And I
placed your there. You were on the holy mountain of
God; You walked in the midst of the stones of fire.
15 "You were blameless in your ways From the day
you were created, Until unrighteousness was found
in you.
16 "By the abundance of your trade You were inter-
nally filled with violence, And you sinned; Therefore I have cast you as profane From the mountain of God. And I have destroyed you, O covering
cherub, from the midst of the stones of fire.
17 "Your heart was lifted up because of your beauty;
You corrupted your wisdom by reason of your
splendor. I cast you to the ground; I put you before
kings, That they may see you.
18 "By the multitude of your iniquities, In the unrighteousness of your trade, You profaned your sanctu-

aries. Therefore I have brought fire from the midst of you; It has consumed you, And I have turned you to ashes on the earth In the eyes of all who see you.

19 "All who know you among the peoples Are appalled at you; You have become terrified, And you will be no more."

In Isaiah 14, the passage also begins with a taunt against the King of Babylon, then, in verse 12, shifts to the "star of the morning" who has fallen from heaven. His five time repeated statement "I will" is a declaration of his will over God's will; his intention to overtake and depose the One True God of heaven. Isaiah 14:12-17:

12 "How you have fallen from heaven, O star of the morning, son of the dawn! You have been cut down to the earth, You have weakened the nations!

13 "But you said in your heart, 'I will ascend to heaven; I will raise my throne above the stars of God, And I will sit on the mount of assembly In the recesses of the north.

14 'I will ascend above the heights of the clouds; I will make myself like the Most High.'

15 "Nevertheless you will be thrust down to Sheol, To the recesses of the pit.

16 "Those who see you will gaze at you, They will ponder over you, saying 'Is this the man who made the earth tremble, Who shook kingdoms,

> **17** Who made the world like a wilderness And overthrew its cities, Who did not allow his prisoners to go home?'

From Ezekiel 28 and this passage, it is apparent Lucifer originated sin through pride, rebellion, and apostasy. This diabolical coup recruited others of the angelic host as one third were swept away and cast to earth (Revelation 12:4). Jesus bore testimony of the devil's fall in Luke 10:18 where He told the 70 disciples who had just returned from a mission of preaching and exorcism that He witnessed Satan fall like lightning from heaven, thus beginning the age-old struggle between good and evil. Not content with the heavenly havoc he had already inaugurated, his next move was to draw man, the capstone of God's creation, into apostasy as he continued his quest for world dominance.

Imagine Adam and Eve, created perfectly in the image of God, dwelling in a perfect garden, in perfect fellowship with one another, and with the Creator Himself. Imagine two human beings so pure they literally walked in the cool of the morning with their holy God.

But then, enter the tempter.

The position the first man and woman had with their Lord was one of complete faith, obedience, and trust. His Word was clearly understood by two humans of perfect intelligence. And yet, Satan was able to appeal to Eve's emotions (Genesis 3:6), where she saw the fruit of the tree of the knowledge of good and evil as: 1) good for food (lust of the flesh), 2) a delight to the eyes (lust of the eyes) and, 3) desirable to make one wise (pride of life), (1st John 2:16). Tragically, the devil used Eve's emotions to deceive her, even worse, when she gave the fruit to Adam, he volitionally sinned with eyes wide open, bringing condemnation to all his descendants thereafter. The seeds of apostasy were sown. When individuals become apostate, whole families, groups, cultures, and eventually nations, fall away. The Bible is replete with examples.

God's Word basically uses four terms when speaking about apostasy: *rebellion, turning away, falling away,* and *adultery.* Old Testament Israel is the primary object lesson regarding it. A nation chosen by Jehovah that had just experienced a miraculous deliverance from slavery, saw the Red Sea part, and stood safely by when Pharaoh's army was destroyed, found itself at the foot of Mount Sinai. It was here God chose to deliver His moral law to Moses. The Bible tells us he ascended the mountain to meet the Lord, but within 40 days the people turned away, making themselves a golden calf to worship. As a result, the Levites were commanded to strike down the idolatrous offenders, and Exodus 32:35 says: "The Lord smote the people, because of what they did with the calf which Aaron had made."

Israel's constant grumbling and complaining regarding food and water during their travels to Canaan became quite tedious. Were it not for the continuous intercession of Moses on their behalf, the Lord would have blotted them out. The final straw for that generation came when the 12 spies made their reconnaissance of the Promised Land. Ten of the twelve issued a fearful report concerning the military capability of the indigenous population, striking terror into the heart of Israel.

Because of their fear and faithlessness, Jehovah pronounced judgment upon all adults twenty years and older. Their bodies would litter the wilderness for the next 40 years. As for the ten spies who rebelled against God's plan for conquest, they were immediately struck down by a plague before the Lord (Numbers 14:26-38).

The bad actors of that generation continued to act badly. Short on water at Meribah, the people complained again. A frustrated Moses struck the rock rather than speaking to it and lost his right to enter Canaan.

Short on food in their detour around Edom, the people complained once more and were chastised by fiery serpents. Then, at Shittim, Balac, the Moabite king, enlisted a prophet named Baalam to curse Israel, but after three attempts, ended up blessing them instead. In the end, all he could do was advise the king to compromise Israel in idolatry. Moabite women were sent to the camp with an invitation to worship Baal Peor in exchange for sexual favors. That particular apostasy cost Israel 24,000 lives by the time Phineas was able to stop the plague with his spear (Numbers 31:16; Revelation 2:14).

From this point, Israel walked the straight and narrow for a time. Unfortunately, Moses' last words to the nation in Deuteronomy entailed both a blessing and a curse and a prediction of future apostasy: "I call heaven and earth to witness against you today, that I have placed before you life and death, the blessing and the curse. So choose life in order that you may live, you and your descendants, by loving the Lord your God, by obeying His voice, and by holding close to Him; for this is your life and the length of your days, so that you may live in the land which the Lord swore to your fathers, to Abraham, Isaac, and Jacob, to give to them" (Deuteronomy 30:19, 20). "The Lord said to Moses, 'Behold, you are about to lie down with your fathers; and this people will arise and play the prostitute with the foreign gods of the land into the midst of which they are going, and they will abandon Me and break my covenant which I have made with them. Then My anger will be kindled against them on that day, and I will abandon them and hide My face from them, and they will be consumed, and many evils and troubles will find them; so they will say on that day, 'Is it not because our God is not among us that these evils have found us?' But I will assuredly hide my face on that day because of all the evil that they will have done, for they will have turned away to other gods'" (Deuteronomy 31:16-18).

General Joshua led the people through a lengthy and miraculous campaign in Canaan. Yet, only about 30% of the promised territory was taken and the pagan peoples who lived there were not completely eradicated. Consequently, they became a snare to Israel. Idolatry became prevalent during the time of the judges "after another generation arose who did not know the Lord nor the work which He had done for Israel" (Judges 2:10). The cycle of faith, to prosperity, to idolatry, to judgment, to repentance, back to faith, was repeated time and again all the way through the dynasties of both Israel's and Judah's kings.

David was a man after God's own heart, but the heart of his son Solomon was turned to his many foreign wives: "And he had seven hundred wives, princesses, and three hundred concubines, and his wives turned his heart away… And Solomon did what was evil in the sight of the Lord, and did not follow the Lord fully, as his father David had done" (1st Kings 11:3, 6).

A king listed as the wisest and wealthiest to ever live, a king who was privileged to build and dedicate Jehovah's temple, who heard directly from God, still fell away from his first love. He would soon be followed by other kings both in Israel and Judah who built shrines and worshiped the at the altars of Baal and Ashtoreth. Eventually, Manasseh, the most idolatrous of all, took power in Judah. This apostate went above and beyond the rest. 2nd Chronicles 33:1-7:

> 1 Manasseh was twelve years old when he became king, and he reigned for fifty-five years in Jerusalem.
> 2 He did evil in the sight of the Lord according to the abominations of the nations whom the Lord disposed before the sons of Israel.
> 3 For he built the high places which his father Hezekiah had torn down; he also set up altars for the Baals and made Asherim, and he worshiped all the heavenly lights and served them.
> 4 He built altars in the house of the Lord of which the Lord had said, "My name shall be in Jerusalem forever."
> 5 He built altars for all the heavenly lights in the two courtyards of the house of the Lord.
> 6 He also made his sons pass through the fire in the valley of Ben-hinnom; and he practiced witchcraft, used divination, practiced sorcery, and dealt with

mediums and spiritists. He did much evil in the sight of the Lord, provoking Him to anger.

7 Then he put the carved image of the idol which he had made in the house of God, of which God had said to David and his son Solomon, "In this house and in Jerusalem, which I have chosen from all the tribes of Israel, I will put My name forever;

Amazingly, this worst of the worst was humbled by captivity in Assyria. But there he repented of his wickedness, returned to Judah, and led his people back to the Lord (2nd Chronicles 33:10-13). Manasseh proved our God is "longsuffering toward us, not willing that any should perish but that all should come to repentance" (2nd Peter 3:9).

With the long view in mind, we can see how Satan attempted to destroy Israel and keep God's promised Redeemer from entering the world scene. The Lord's judgment for Israel's apostasy would culminate in a 70 year Babylonian captivity followed by subjugation to the succeeding gentile empires of Medo-Persia, Greece, and Rome.

As stated earlier, individual apostasy eventually leads to national apostasy of which Israel is the world's object lesson. Again, this was the concern of America's early founders as they watched the light of the "City on a Hill" grow dim. But the Great Awakening led by Edwards, the Wesleys, Whitefield and others, under the unction of God the Holy Spirit, put some light back into the city and laid the Christian foundation upon which our Constitution would be framed. Though often argued, it really is beyond debate that the faith heritage of the United States is Christian. If that is true, and we know it is, America has held a unique and privileged position on the world stage for its entire existence. For nearly a quarter-millennia, this nation, founded on Christian principle by Christian men, has enjoyed the blessings of God as well as His divine protection. We have endured revolution, depression, recession, civil war, world wars, and so called "limited wars." Unfortunately, it appears that what external threats could not accomplish, internal threats likely will. And, I would say it is only since the Lord has begun to withdraw His protecting hand that domestic threats actually pose a clear and present danger. Why would God do that to us, we the people of the United Sates of America? For the same reason He did it to Israel – apostasy.

Though the U.S. was for some time culturally Christian, it no longer is. The biblical world view once generally held that included the Golden Rule "Do unto others as you would have them do unto you" and "Just as you want people to treat you, treat them in the same way" (Matthew 7:12; Luke 6:31) is barely noticeable. Today, modern America does not live by the Golden Rule, the Great Commandment, or the Great Commission, but follows the path of secularism and self. These are false gods in opposition to the One True God of Heaven. These gods are not only at enmity with Christ but celebrate their rebellion against Him. Sexual immorality, a burgeoning pornography industry, and the perversion of transgenderism are being pushed as *normal* behavior in our wayward society. Freedoms guaranteed under the Constitution and Bill of Rights are abused, facilitating vulgarity, drunkenness, drug abuse, promiscuity, abortion, and violence. Greed, the besetting sin of America, and most of the world, seems to be the cause of much of it. Paul accurately declared in 1st Timothy 6:10: "For the love of money is a root of all sorts of evil, and some longing for it have wandered away from the faith and pierced themselves with many a pang."

Somehow, with the abandonment of godly values and blatant indifference to our omnipotent Creator, we still expect Him to shower us with blessing. Lee Greenwood's "God Bless the USA" was composed in 1984 and has been performed at significant political events, beginning with the 1984 Republican National Convention and upon our entry into the first Gulf War. I love the song, but now when I hear it, I find myself asking, "Why should God bless the USA?" Morally and spiritually compromised, we have no merit for which we should be blessed. To turn our backs on Him, then demand blessing from Him, is foolish arrogance that stems from self-interest and a serious misunderstanding of the person and character of God.

I remember growing up in the public education system of yesteryear. Before the first lesson began, our teachers led us in prayer followed by the Pledge. Then we began our studies in the "3 Rs" – Reading, Writing, and 'Rithmatic. These basics were augmented by American history and civics, emphasizing patriotic values. We sang "God Bless America" in music class and never doubted that He really did exist! Though we were a long way away from the classical education of our Founders, we flourished in the absence of woke, evolutionary, and CRT indoctrination.

So, we find that education is another area in which we have fallen away from a position once held. William Tennent, the Presbyterian minister mentioned earlier who sparked a revival in his own church, also founded the Log College in Westminster, Pennsylvania. His graduates became powerful revivalist preachers in the Great Awakening. George Whitefield described the physical structure of the Log College as "very plain, though highly innovative." That primitive theological college was renamed in 1896 "Princeton University." Today, the opiate of secularism has erased much of the memory of how America's educational institutions began, hiding the fact that 98% of the first 108 early colleges were famously Christian. Now, most so-called *Christian* colleges are anything but.

Co-author of the First Amendment, Fisher Ames, made a cogent observation regarding American education way back in 1789: "We have a dangerous trend beginning to take place in our education. We're starting to put more and more textbooks in our schools. We've become accustomed to putting little books into the hands of children, containing fables and moral lessons. We're spending less time in the classroom on the Bible, which should be the primary text in our schools." Imagine that – a period in our history where the King James Bible was the main textbook! The average secular socialist, who likely never learned any of these things in the public indoctrination centers, would go apoplectic if he knew the real foundation of this land.

America's cultural perversion was hastened by a compromised Supreme Court. The rulings of Engle v. Vitale in 1962, removing prayer from school, and the 1963 decision, Abington School District v. Schempp, barring Bible reading and the Lord's Prayer in school, started us down a slippery slope. The U.S. government formally made the principal textbook of our ancestors, the Holy Bible, into something illegal - and we expect God to bless the USA?

The church is the church, and the government is the government, but common sense tells us our Constitutional Republic was created to be governed from a biblical world view. John Adams explained this in 1798: "We have no government armed with power capable of contending with human passions unbridled by morality and religion. Avarice, ambition, revenge, or gallantry, would break the strongest cords of our Constitution as a whale goes through a net. Our Constitution was made only for a moral and religious [Adam's word for *Christian*] people. It is wholly inadequate to the government of any other."

George Washington's prayer contained in a letter written in 1783, stated: "That [God] would most graciously be pleased to dispose us all to do Justice, to love mercy, and to demean ourselves with that Charity, humility, and pacific temper of mind, which were the Characteristics of the Divine Author of our blessed Religion, and without an humble imitation of whose example in these things, we can never hope to be a happy Nation."

Again, the term "religion" as used by the Founders meant Christianity. It is conveniently used today by non-believers, and those who would mitigate our forefather's intentions, to mean *all* religions. Obviously, that was not the intent, in fact, other religions such as Islam, Hinduism, including atheism (which is a religion), reject and oppose Judeo-Christian principles the US Constitution takes for granted. Our war with Islamic terrorism for the last two decades makes this apparent, even though soft-headed virtue signalers insist the murder cult of Islam be incorporated into our Republic.

National apostasy occurred in Israel when she abandoned her faith in Jehovah and embraced the pagan gods of the surrounding nations. Like Israel, the United States has forsaken the faith of her fathers, leaving a void that will be filled by something else. That something else is a host of false deities offered by the world, the flesh, and the devil. It is those demonic substitutes I would like to examine next.

CHAPTER 3

Causes of Apostasy

The last chapter focused on national apostasy with our emphasis more upon the foundations that have been abandoned than causes of the abandonment. The problems of our world are usually couched in terms material and horizontal in that human beings generally see things lineally and not vertically. This viewpoint puts us at an immediate disadvantage because we know the first step in solving any problem is to identify it. The problems of America and the world are spiritual, not material, all of them having an underlying spiritual cause. Thus, they can only be identified by spiritual perception, or "spiritual eyes" if you will. The dilemma in which we find ourselves is that, by and large, we have no spiritual perception. Paul reminds us in 1st Corinthians 2:14: "But a natural man does not accept the things of the Spirit of God; for they are foolishness to him, and he cannot understand them, because they are spiritually appraised."

The natural man is an unspiritual man, one who has not been born again by the Spirit of God – which is the majority of the world's population. We really can't fault unspiritual people for not being able to see a spiritual problem, for they do not possess the apparatus to do so. On the other hand, scripture makes it clear that all are without excuse: "For since the creation of the world His invisible attributes, His eternal power and divine nature, have been clearly seen, being understood through what has been made, so that they are without excuse" (Romans 1:20). The Bible says here that the General Revelation given to man in God's creation is enough to direct him to spiritual inquiry, but most ignore the prompting. So, like our first father and mother in the Garden, all men everywhere are without excuse. Nevertheless, the problems remain spiritual and must be overcome with spiritual weapons.

We have already seen that the first instigator of spiritual conflict was a spirit being named Lucifer, the guardian cherub who became Satan (adversary), and the devil (slanderer or accuser). He is seen consistently throughout God's Word under various names. A partial list includes: Abaddon, Angel of the Abyss, Apollyon (Revelation 9:11); Beelzebul (Matthew 12:24); Belial (2nd Corinthians 6:15); god of this world (2nd Corinthians 4:4); Prince of the Power of the Air (Ephesians 2:2); Serpent (Genesis 3:4); and Evil One (Matthew 13:19). The reality of the existence of this deadly, implacable foe is evidenced all through scripture, and the reason God crafted a plan for man's salvation. Still, most do not believe in his existence. Of course, Satan's best weapon against man is the notion that he does not exist; that he is just a medieval fairy tale with red horns and a pitchfork. But his existence is taken seriously in the Holy Writ.

God was very direct when He told the devil in Genesis 3:15, "And I will put enmity between you and the woman, And between your seed and her seed; He shall bruise you on the head, And you shall bruise Him on the heel." The adversary understood exactly what God meant, and from that point forward has done all he can to derail God's plan.

First, he orchestrated Cain's murder of Abel (Genesis 4:8), then, the corrupting of the line of Seth (Genesis 6:1-12), the attempted rapes of Sarah and Rebekah (Genesis 12:10-20; 20:1-18), Rebekah's plan to cheat Esau out of his birthright, creating a murderous hostility in Esau against Jacob (Genesis 27), the murder of Israel's male children in Egypt (Exodus 1:15-22), the attempted murders of David (1st Samuel 18:10, 11), Queen Athalia's effort to destroy the royal seed (2nd Chronicle 22:10), Haman's plot to slaughter the Jews (Esther 3:9), and the constant drawing of Israel into idolatry to sacrifice their children in pagan rituals (Leviticus 18; 2nd Kings 16; 2nd Chronicles 28; Psalm 106; Ezekiel 16, and numerous other places).

In the New Testament, wicked King Herod, inspired by Satan, murdered the children of Bethlehem in an intentional effort to thwart God's plan (Matthew 2:16). Next, the devil showed up in person to try and compromise Jesus in the wilderness of temptation (Matthew 4). Then we find satanically inspired religious legalists constantly attacking the ministry and person of Christ, which eventually led to their success in taking His life at the cross.

The conflict we face is spiritual and eternal. It is a broad battle, spanning both heaven and earth, involving both men and angels. Yet, as apparent as it is to those with spiritual eyes, most of the planet remains oblivious. People, particularly in the West, really do not believe such evil exists. They willfully choose not to recognize the malevolent intentions of Satan and his followers. But he is here, and evil is real, and is the reason for the current gross insanity engulfing our planet.

Satan's demons have long been at work in America, their activities undercover for the most part, as the devil performed spiritual espionage on our Christian Republic. Most of Europe capitulated to him long ago. The continents of Asia, Africa, South America, and Australia have largely been his, except for the few Christian inroads made over the centuries. Believers in these places are now savagely persecuted. However, the United States, positioned on the continent of North America, was created as "one nation under God." Herein lay the challenge. She was the City on a Hill, shining light into Satanic darkness, the last hope of true liberty on the globe. She was a force to be reckoned with, a formidable opponent to a being whose goal was to become like the Most-High God and usurp the very throne of heaven. This nation stood in the way of his global conquest only because godly people in faithful churches across our land interceded before the throne of grace. This obstacle to his world domination had to be removed at all costs. So, the forces of hell were marshalled against her. Yet, when she donned the full armor of God, lifting up the shield of faith and bearing the sword of the Spirit (the Word of God), she was able to quench his fiery darts and resist his attacks. But the devil's arsenal was broad.

His weapons of complacency, self-focus, and greed were parasitic larvae deposited within the blessings of God. As they matured, they weakened their host, eroded the armor and dulled the sword. As they multiplied, they diminished her health, affecting her vision (Proverbs 29:18) and her hearing (Amos 8:11). Adding to her destruction, she sought remedies apart from the Great Physician – remedies offered by others who posed as healers. Her faithlessness moved her out from under the protection and provision of the One who cared for her. She became vulnerable and weak, and the devil rejoiced.

For the last one hundred years the doctrines of demons have found their way, not only into secular society, but into the Church itself, chipping away at its foundations: "But the Spirit explicitly says that in later times some will fall away from the faith, paying attention to deceitful spirits and teachings of demons, by means of the hypocrisy of liars seared in their own conscience as with a branding iron, who forbid marriage and advocate abstaining from foods which God has created to be gratefully shared in by those who believe and know the truth" (1st Timothy 3:1-3).

Paul told Pastor Timothy that the Holy Spirit specifically said in the "later times" there would be a falling away precipitated by demonic doctrines. What might some of those doctrines (teachings) be? He names a couple of them, listing forbidding marriage and abstaining from foods, both of which God created for the benefit of man. We would call this religious self-denial, or asceticism, i.e., doing works to merit God's favor, or generate holiness (Titus 3:5). Another demonic doctrine that has pervaded the church is religious formalism – exercising ritualism without any Holy Spirit power. Others prevalent today are, the departure from historic orthodox faith and adding to, or subtracting from God's inspired Word. And then, there is the sort of false teaching like John spoke of in his letters which denied Jesus Christ had actually come in the flesh. In the last book of the Bible, Christ Himself addressed false teachers and teaching that had already crept into the church through one "Jezebel," the Nicolaitans, and the teaching of Balaam, seen in Revelation 2.

These aberrations from true Bible faith have come at great cost to the universal church generally, and the American church specifically. In Europe, magnificent Christian cathedrals have been turned into mosques, community centers, and stores. Here, many American congregations are on life support. Today, a fellowship of 100 people is considered a *large* church. Buildings that once accommodated hundreds or thousands in gospel meetings, now operate at a fraction of their capacity. But even those that remain true to the Word and have not compromised are often ignored or marginalized.

I semi-retired four years ago and moved to a new home near Saginaw, Michigan. During these four years, my wife and I have diligently sought a church home, unfortunately, without success. All we are looking for is the Word of God to be properly taught in the power of His Spirit, which seems nearly impossible to find. Forty years in the pulpit almost every Sunday did not allow me to get out and observe the generational sea change that was happening. I feel kind of like Rip Van-Winkle, waking up to a new reality. From my observation, I can only ask: "Is it any wonder America is in trouble?" It has been said that as the Church goes, so goes the world. This was true during the Great Awakening and true now again during our current Great Apostasy.

The problem is spiritual. Satan, in his subtlety, has hijacked the country. Though he has been at it since the beginning, he has only recently achieved his greatest success. Personally, I believe the watershed moment came during the fraudulent presidential election of 2020, though the purloining has been going on for decades. Yes, according to the left, I am an "election denier," but I only deny dishonest elections. There is plenty of evidence to support what we all know. But crooked elections are not the scope of this chapter, only a contributing factor to the Satanic overthrow currently in progress.

Four years previous, another usurper was in line for her coronation, but the powers in control at that time made some huge miscalculations. All the necessary steps required to keep Donald Trump out of the White House were not taken. Consequently, a four-year economic revival, energy independence, and peace on the world stage broke out that did not serve the socialist agenda. So, for four years, tactical and strategic operations were conducted against an innocent Patriot President and the U.S. Constitution. Lie after lie, impeachment after impeachment, and lawfare after lawfare were perpetrated against a man who was only guilty of loving his country. When those efforts failed, the next thing had to be assassination. Likely, the attempt made on July 13, 2024, against the 45th President will not be the last as corrupt government, foreign powers, and a biased mainstream media continue their collusion. We sometimes hear pundits express wonder at the duplicity of the media, yet scripture assures us the devil is "the prince of the power of the air, the spirit that is now working in the children of disobedience" (Ephesians 2:2). The media in all its forms is completely controlled by the enemy.

It appears Satan vowed never to let a 2016 happen again, and, by 2020, he had all the right forces staged in all the right places. November 3rd was a spiritual D-Day. Unfortunately, the armies of good stood flat-footed on the beach, not expecting the onslaught, or ignoring it if they did. Compromised election boards, voting machines controlled by foreign nations connected to the internet, and federal agencies in support, were all well positioned by their master. Satan's mask finally came off, even though his henchmen insisted U.S. citizens wear theirs, remain six feet apart (the depth of a grave), and did not associate with one another.

The planned-demic was another handy weapon employed against our Constitutional Republic by elites who relish power and control. Unending tyrannical lockdowns of both citizens and businesses nearly buried us economically. Those in authority got to pick and choose who was allowed to make a living, and who wasn't. Usually, it was the small business owner, the mom-and-pop shop that suffered most and eventually closed. But we know free enterprise is anathema to Marxist/communist philosophy. Heads of the alphabet agencies FBI, CIA, NSA, DHS, etc. (known communist sympathizers appointed by the Obama administration) combined their efforts in the Russian Dossier hoax in an effort to depose a duly elected president. Those efforts eventually failed as Satan's swamp became more exposed. But he is relentless.

An easily manipulated dementia victim was found who could be kept in a basement out of sight during the 2020 campaign cycle. This man only surfaced on occasion to reassure the American electorate that their taxes were not going to go down, but up; that he planned to shut down all fossil fuel production, and intended to disarm the population. He also planned to re-enter harmful treaties with our enemies and open our borders to anyone and everyone, while at the same time, dismantling local police departments. This "winning" platform was supposedly approved by the greatest margin of voters in American history!

Sure… and for four years now, deceptive gaslighting worsens by the day, as does American misery. Elections have consequences, and stolen elections by demonically inspired criminals have dire consequences. The conflict is spiritual.

It was idolatry that brought Israel to judgment, and so it is with the United States. The problem with idols is that they are backed by demons (1st Corinthians 10:20, 21). Most Western pseudo-sophisticates deny they are idol worshipers, imagining figures cast in silver and gold. But isn't that what is still worshiped today? We may not mold our precious metals into miniature likenesses of humans or animals, however, we do form idols in the shape of IRAs, checking accounts, stocks, bonds, real estate, and other assets. In fact, we worship at the altar of the bronze bull of Wall Street, not unlike the golden calf of the children of Israel. Idolatry is whatever takes precedence over the Lord. The first commandment of the Ten says: "You shall have no other gods before me" (Exodus 20:3). But human beings have found a plethora of other things with which to replace God. We worship Satan indirectly when we do. Yet, that indirect worship seems to become more direct every day.

The Satanic Temple recently opened a new headquarters in Salem, Massachusetts (of course). Among the various art forms there, dedicated to the devil, is a seven feet tall bronze of the goat-headed demon, Baphomet, with children looking up to him. The curators say the Satanic Temple is primarily devoted to political causes, like the separation of church and state! It is disturbing that Satanism and other forms of idolatry are effectively reaching down to our youth.

I was flabbergasted when my fourteen-year-old granddaughter related how numbers of her peers were allowed to attend school with eccentric and abnormal clothing and hair styles. As she spoke, I wondered how a teacher could maintain enough order and discipline to be able to teach a class. She went on to describe how kids decorate themselves with occult symbols, like one who painted a pentagram on her forehead. When questioned about it, the girl replied it was a protection symbol given to her by Baal! The hair stood up on my neck when I heard this clear endorsement of the Canaanite fertility god responsible for the debauchery and downfall of Israel. My granddaughter, a young girl of strong faith, also said there was open hostility directed toward students who follow Christ. This is public middle school.

The conflict is spiritual, and there is a battle raging for the souls of our children. Don't you think it odd that today's school boards want to take ownership of our kids and label parents domestic terrorists? Honestly, I am concerned for the safety of my granddaughter, especially when I hear about experimentation in homosexuality and gender dysphoria encouraged by adults in the school system.

In the recent tragic slaughter of three nine-year-olds and three adults at Covenant Presbyterian School in Nashville, we witnessed the culmination of transgender insanity. We saw a deliberate targeting of Christians by a person who did not like the viewpoint of Christianity that says "male and female created He them" (Genesis 1:27; 5:2). Make no mistake, hatred for Jesus Christ and His followers is real. The disdain for all things Christian, including the founding tenants of our nation, is actual and growing. It is a top-down influence, starting with the devil himself. Jesus warned us, predicting persecution would be our lot in this life (John 15:20, and several other places). With church buildings all around us, we have taken "church" for granted in the U.S. From the earliest settlers, it has been a part of our culture. But I find most American Christians don't realize our largely un-persecuted faith is the exception and not the rule.

The American church is an anomaly in the two-thousand year history of Christianity. Voice of the Martyrs and other organizations tell us the 20th century saw more persecution of Christians worldwide than any century previous. The world is now well on its way to surpassing that record just twenty-four years into this one. It appears the U.S. government intends to add to those statistics as well. Just look at how the church was threatened during the COVID scam-demic. Deemed "non-essential," local assemblies were threatened with fines, and congregants with arrest for obeying the biblical mandate: "not forsaking our own assembling together" (Hebrews 10:25), and Peter's words: "We must obey God rather than men" (Acts 5:29).

I was sorely disappointed in the cowardly compliance of the Church during the lockdowns. Nowhere in its history, during plagues, pestilence, and disease has the Church closed its doors – except here. It wasn't even the presence of a virus that shuttered most of them, but the mere threat of it. What the devil could not do with dungeon, fire, and sword, on other continents, he accomplished here with just a little intimidation. We need to re-study 2nd Timothy 1:7: "For God hath not given us the spirit of fear; but of power, and of love, and of a sound mind" (KJV). Many bodies now regret their choice to close during COVID because a significant number of churchgoers who quit attending services then, never returned. The devil is pretty crafty, isn't he?

Why is the government so determined to see the Christian church disappear? Bottom line is that government wants to be God. There is no room in a Marxist, communist, globalist dictatorship for the God of the Bible because He is opposed to their godless agenda and always has been. So, subtly, and not so subtly, the Lord has been squeezed out of government, out of school, out of business, out of the public square, out of many churches, and out of our lives, while we stood by and watched complacently. Unlike Freylingheuzen, Tennet, Edwards, and Whitefield, who stood up to the wiles of the devil, we found it easier to just retreat into our comfort zone.

In the book of Revelation, Jesus addressed the seven representative churches which are types of congregations that existed then and now. Only two out of the seven received no criticism from the Lord – Smyrna, the persecuted church, and Philadelphia, the church of witness and brotherly love.

I know most churches today claim to be Philadelphian, however, I believe, in this country, most are closer to Laodicea: "So because you are lukewarm, and neither hot nor cold, I will spit (vomit) you out of My mouth" (Revelation 3:16).

Yes, the fat, dumb and happy American church is pretty gag-worthy. And until it starts standing up, and praying up, and preaching up, and speaking up, and looking up, returning to that "old-time religion," becoming the church militant once again – storming the gates of hell, like we're supposed to – Satan will just continue to run his game.

The conflict is spiritual. It must be fought with spiritual weapons (2nd Corinthians 10:4). Time to don our battle gear before it's too late.

CHAPTER 4

Spiritual Control of Nations

We spent a majority of the last chapter demonstrating the control principalities and powers have over this country. I know there are those who will never see it that way, but you must have spiritual eyes to see it. The Bible gives a clear picture of, not only the way Israel was affected by demonic influence, but succeeding gentile world empires as well.

Israel dispossessed the Canaanite peoples because of their demonic degeneracy, even though God gave them space to repent as revealed to Abraham in Genesis 15:16. The Bible shows us how Satan attempted to destroy the Jewish nation through bondage in Egypt and in the following wilderness experience. Eventually, after centuries of waffling between faith and unbelief, revival and apostasy, the remnant of Judah was dragged into captivity. Babylon was the chosen instrument of God to destroy Jerusalem in 586 BC. The ten northern tribes had already been laid waste by Assyria in 722 BC.

In Nebuchadnezzar's first attack on Jerusalem in 605 BC, a young man named Daniel was taken captive, deported to Babylon and made a court eunuch. He would be God's chosen vessel to draw Jehovah's prophetic roadmap to the end of the age.

In Daniel, chapter 2, King Nebuchadnezzar had a dream that so disturbed him, he immediately called for all the soothsayers and master astrologers of the land, demanding an interpretation. The problem was that the King not only demanded an interpretation, but required a recounting of the dream as well. This impossibility drove everyone into a panic because Nebuchadnezzar decreed death to all the wise men in the empire if they didn't come up with it. This was a call to prayer for Daniel and his friends Shadrach, Meshach, and Abednego.

After seeking God's face in the matter, the Lord revealed to Daniel both the dream and its interpretation. The prophet then went boldly before the King armed with God's Word. After giving glory to the Lord, Daniel revealed to King Nebuchadnezzar what Jehovah had shown him. Daniel 2:31-45:

> **31** "You, O King, were looking and behold, there was a single great statue; that statue which was large and of extraordinary splendor, was standing in front of you and its appearance was awesome.
>
> **32** "The head of that statue was made of fine gold, its breast and its arms of silver, its belly and its thighs of bronze,
>
> **33** its legs of iron, its feet partly of iron and partly of clay.
>
> **34** "You continued looking until a stone was cut out without hands, and it struck the statue on its feet of iron and clay, and crushed them.

35 "Then the iron, the clay, the bronze, the silver
and the gold were crushed all at the same time,
and became like chaff from the summer threshing
floors; and the wind carried them away so that not
a trace of them was found. But the stone that struck
the statue became a great mountain and filled the
whole earth.
36 "This was the dream; now we shall tell its interpretation before the king.
37 "You O king, are the king of kings, to whom the
God of heaven has given the kingdom, the power,
the strength, and the glory;
38 and wherever the sons of men dwell, or the beasts
of the field, or the birds of the sky, He has given
them into your hand and has caused you to rule
over them all. You are the head of gold.
39 "And after you there will arise another kingdom
inferior to you, then another third kingdom of
bronze, which will rule over all the earth.
40 "Then there will be a fourth kingdom as strong
as iron; inasmuch as iron crushes and shatters all
things, so, like iron that breaks in pieces, it will
crush and break all these in pieces.
41 "And in that you saw the feet and toes, partly of
clay and partly of iron, it will be a divided kingdom; but it will have in it the toughness of iron,
inasmuch as you saw the iron mixed with common
clay.

42 "And as the toes of the feet were partly of iron and partly of pottery, so some of the kingdom will be strong and part of it will be brittle.
43 "And in that you saw the iron mixed with common clay, they will combine with one another in the seed of men; but they will not adhere to one another, even as iron does not combine with pottery.
44 "And in the days of those kings the God of heaven will set up a kingdom which will never be destroyed, and that kingdom will not be left for another people; it will crush and put an end to all these kingdoms, but it will itself endure forever.
45 "Inasmuch as you saw that a stone was cut out of the mountain without hands and that it crushed the iron, the bronze, the clay, the silver, and the gold, the great God has made known to the king what will take place in the future; so the dream is true, and its interpretation is trustworthy."

It is amazing to me that the Lord chose to reveal eternal truth to a pagan gentile king. Here King Nebuchadnezzar saw, centuries into the future, four additional empires that stretched far beyond his own. The king's image takes us from Babylon – the head of gold, to Medo-Persia – the chest and arms of silver, to Greece – the stomach and thighs of brass, to Rome – legs of iron, and the last gentile kingdom that some call the revived Roman Empire – feet and toes of iron mixed with clay. Nebuchadnezzar's image showed, not only consecutive gentile empires, but amazingly, the earth's final global kingdom, that of Jesus Christ (verses 44, 45).

Daniel's ministry continued through the relatively short-lived Babylonian rule into the succeeding Persian Empire. The book of Daniel is very futuristic in nature, revealing in detail near/far conflicts and intrigues that would take place across the centuries, events that pertained both to Jews and gentiles. There is one place in his writing I would like to revisit to see the spiritual panorama of what is happening in world governments, including our own.

In Daniel, chapter ten, we find the prophet fasting and praying for three weeks as he contemplates the state of his people Israel. An angelic being appeared to him who resembled the description of Christ seen in the book of Revelation. But by verse ten, it appears that another angel, likely Gabriel, the angel he had seen before, came to deliver God's answer. Interestingly, the messenger told him that the moment Daniel bowed himself in prayer, he was dispatched to the prophet. Yet, for 21 days (three weeks) the angel was resisted by the Prince of Persia and was only able to continue once the archangel Michael came to his aid (Daniel 10:13). After reassuring Daniel regarding his people Israel, the angel said he must go back to fight against the prince of Persia and anticipated a battle with the coming prince of Greece, being helped only by Michael.

In Daniel 10:10-21, the curtain is drawn back regarding spiritual warfare that goes on behind the scenes of human history. In this passage we find reference to at least three supernatural beings - two demonic angels and one holy angel - who are powers over Persia, Greece, and Israel. Is it any wonder, then, that the Apostle Paul says "…our struggle is not against flesh and blood, but against the rulers, against the powers, against the world forces of this darkness, against the spiritual forces of wickedness in the heavenly places," (Ephesians 6:12).

The war is spiritual, it is real, and it spans the world. If it is an actual war, then we are soldiers in the fight and Paul exhorts us to put on the full armor for battle (Ephesians 6:13-17). The thing I see most often, however, are troops "absent without leave," (AWOL – US Army, or UA – unauthorized absence, USMC). Christians don't usually view themselves as soldiers on a mission in enemy territory, but rather members of a country club who attend weekly meetings and pay dues whenever they feel like it. Instead of storming the gates of hell and breaking down satanic strongholds, we've taken leave while the enemy surrounds our camp.

From Daniel's writings, we learn that evil principalities and powers have governed world empires since ancient times. The only things that have changed are technology and humans currently alive. Historically, western nations influenced by Christianity were able to stave off complete demonic takeover, America being the most successful. But the devil and his legions have never relented in their campaign for global domination, and it looks like we are in the midst of his final assault.

Obviously, the U.S. has been on Satan's "to do" list for a long time. In the past it was shielded by prayer cover from the New Testament church that thinned as the Church descended into apostasy. As the foundations were chipped away little by little, God's protecting hand has been pulled back accordingly:

Remove prayer from schools – His hand pulled back; Remove the Bible from schools and public institutions – His hand pulled back; Abandon worship and serving the Lord – His hand pulled back even more. And once you have completely eliminated Him from your personal life and the public square, His protecting hand is completely removed (Lamentations 2:3). The world that Satan and the secularists want, devoid of any restraints by a holy and heavenly God, will finally arrive. But neither people nor government can operate in a vacuum. The void will be filled. The demons that were once cast out, rush back in.

American citizens have been bewildered by the overt insanity heaped upon them these last few years. But the "return to normalcy," hoped for by so many, can't happen as long as demons are in the driver's seat and inmates run the asylum.

Messianic Rabbi, Jonathan Cahn, has done extensive research on this topic and wrote a definitive work titled, *The Return of the Gods.* Interestingly, I found his book after beginning to write this one, and was glad to learn his themes and ideas tracked with my own. No doubt the Holy Spirit is trying to get our attention through multiple avenues before judgment falls.

Cahn's well-researched volume makes the case regarding the diabolical conquest Americans are suffering through today. The ancient gods that ensnared Israel, particularly Baal, Ashtoreth, and Molech, have reemerged since the One True God of heaven has been removed. Cahn references a little known teaching of Christ found in Matthew 12:43-45:

43 "Now when the unclean spirit goes out of a man, it passes through waterless places, seeking rest, and does not find it.
44 "Then it says, 'I will return to my house from which I came'; and when it comes, it finds it unoccupied, swept, and put in order.
45 "Then it goes, and takes along with it seven other spirits more wicked than itself, and they go in and live there; and the last state of that man becomes worse than the first. That is the way it will also be with this evil generation."

I have taught through Matthew and exegeted this passage based upon its content concerning an individual who was once demon possessed, and the demon leaving for whatever reason. It appears this person had decided to change his ways, turn over a new leaf, or opt for some kind of self-improvement. The story shows us a room, once occupied by the demon, that had been cleaned and swept. However, nothing was put into the empty space. There was now a void that appealed to the displaced demon who returned to his previous home. Only, this time, there was room enough for seven others more wicked than himself. And so, the man's last state became worse than his first.

At the end of the story, Christ declares the application when He says: "That is the way it will be with this evil generation." I think we can make His application near/far. The generation Jesus spoke to saw the work of Christ in casting out demons. They accepted His healing and saw their room cleaned and swept, yet they did not replace what was driven out. They were satisfied with their own good works and ultimately rejected their Messiah, which soon brought Israel to destruction. That is the near application. The far application can also be made.

Western civilization was blessed to be introduced to Christianity through the colossal efforts of the Apostle Paul. The good news of Christ's gospel replaced the doctrines of demons and pagan gods of Europe, the same gods, by the way, that plagued Israel, only under different names. The Canaanite, Baal, would become the Greek, Zeus, and the Roman, Jupiter. The Canaanite, Ashtoreth, would become the Greek, Aphrodite, and the Roman, Venus. In today's world, we would name them *materialism, greed, sexual immorality* and *perversion.*

Our modern mindset tends to scoff at the idea of ancient gods whom we consider mythical fantasy. We believe these were fables of superstitious people who did things according to their naivete in opposition to science. After all, most church goers today do not believe the Old Testament is a Holy Spirit inspired document given for our spiritual wisdom and understanding. Many think all we need is the New Testament, and only to the extent that it matches our feelings and lifestyle. But the ancient gods, though largely unseen, were real as Paul declared, and behind every idol lurked a demon (1st Corinthians 10:20, 21), and they were still worshiped in the Greco/Roman world.

The name "Baal" means *master and lord.* To the ancients he was the god of prosperity. If you wanted your fields to be fruitful, you sacrificed to Baal. One of his symbols was the bull, a representation of power, prosperity, and fertility. Recall the bronze bull of Wall Street mentioned earlier, and the golden calf of Mount Sinai. America's prevailing idol has long been greed and her children, self-centeredness and materialism – the besetting sins of America, as well as most of the world.

Baal's close consort was Ashtoreth, AKA "Ishtar." She was and is the goddess of sexuality, and the current overseer and instigator of all forms of licentiousness, debauchery, and perversion. Though her spell had been broken by the advance of Christianity in Europe, it is now recast. This alluring goddess presides over the deification of sex. She encourages the severance of sex from the bonds of marriage into any and all deviance. The sexual rites, once performed in her temples and shrines by past devotees, have become mainstream in American culture. Today, she encourages promiscuity, prostitution, pornography, pedophilia, homosexuality, beastiality, transgenderism, and anything else the fallen sin nature can invent. Activities that were once illegal and shocking, have become legal and familiar. This familiarity has led to numbness, which has led to tolerance and acceptance. Sin that was once condemned is now celebrated and made a matter of "pride."

Jonathan Cahn makes an interesting point in his book regarding the timing of these perversions. As I write, we are entering the month of June, a month important to the festivals of Ishtar, dubbed "pride month" around the world. As Ishtar was also the goddess of pride, the title is fitting. For years we were forced to observe "Gay Pride Day," then "Gay Pride Week," until she fully regained control of her favorite month,

June, also the month of the summer solstice. On the Hebrew calendar, it is the month of Tammuz. June was, in pagan mythology, the month Ashtoreth mourned for her lost lover, Tammuz. Ezekiel was given a vision of apostate Judah weeping for Tammuz during this time (Ezekiel 8:14). Our country celebrates patriotic holidays on single days of the year, but Ishtar/Ashtoreth gets 29 days upon which her followers are encouraged to practice sexual deviation of every kind.

It is important to note that landmark Supreme Court decisions were ratified during this month. Which landmark decisions? On June 26th, 2003, in *Lawrence vs. Texas*, the U.S. Supreme Court legalized homosexuality throughout the land. On June 26th, 2013, the Supreme Court ruled against the Defense of Marriage Act in *U.S. vs. Windsor.* On June 26th, 2015, SCOTUS ruled on *Obergefell vs. Hodges,* requiring all states to recognize same sex marriage. Notice, all three of these major decisions fell on the same date, toward the end of June – the time apostate women in Jerusalem wept for Ishtar's lover, Tammuz. Truly, this perverse goddess is having her way in America. Yet, there was one spark of light in all of this darkness that occurred in June. On the 24th of that month, 2022, the Supreme Court overturned the infamous *Roe vs. Wade* decision of 1973, much to the ire of Ishtar.

In league with Baal and Ashtoreth was the dark god of the Amorites, Molech. He was particularly evil in that he required human sacrifice. Molech was so abhorrent, Jehovah gave stern warning to the Israelites who entered his territory. Leviticus 20:2-5:

> **2** "You shall also say to the sons of Israel, 'Any man from the sons of Israel or from the aliens sojourning in Israel, who gives any of his offspring to Molech, shall surely be put to death; the people of the land shall stone him with stones.
> **3** 'I will also set my face against that man and will cut him off from among his people, because he has given some of his offspring to Molech, so as to defile my sanctuary and to profane my holy name.'"

The revulsion of this idol was the sacrifice of children in fire by their own parents, strictly forbidden in Deuteronomy 18:10 and other places. Yet, when Israel and Judah fell away from Jehovah in apostasy, the demons of Baal, Ashtoreth, and Molech quickly returned.

In my reading of the Old Testament, I find it disturbing that the bulk of Israel's idolatry happened under its kings, both north and south. Solomon, son of David, wisest and richest man who ever lived, writer of scripture and builder of the Lord's temple, bears much of the guilt. 1st Kings 11:1-7 says this:

> **1** Now King Solomon loved many foreign women along with the daughter of Pharaoh: Moabite, Ammonite, Edomite, Sidonian, and Hittite women,
> **2** from the nations concerning which the Lord had said to the sons of Israel, "You shall not associate with them, neither shall they associate with you, for they will surely turn your heart away after their gods." Solomon held fast to these in love.

3 And he had seven hundred wives, princesses, and three hundred concubines, and his wives turned his heart away.

4 For it came about when Solomon was old, his wives turned his heart away after other gods; and his heart was not wholly devoted to the Lord his God, as the heart of David his father had been.

5 For Solomon went after Ashtoreth the goddess of the Sidonians and after Milcom the detestable idol of the Ammonites.

6 And Solomon did what was evil in the sight of the Lord, and did not follow the Lord fully, as David his father had done.

7 Then Solomon built a high place for Chemosh the detestable idol of Moab, on the mountain which is east of Jerusalem, and for Molech the detestable idol of the sons of Ammon.

When scripture says they "burned incense and offered sacrifice to their gods," it means they offered their children to Molech by fire. Solomon gave himself to Ashtoreth, the goddess of sexual perversion, evidenced by seven hundred foreign wives and three hundred concubines. They were the ones who turned his heart away in apostasy. Thirteen kings later, after bouncing back and forth between apostasy and revival, between good kings and bad kings, Manasseh was born. This monarch exceeded all others in his dedication to the false gods of Baal, Ashtoreth, and Molech, plunging Judah into the worst apostasy, yet. 2nd Chronicles 33:1-9 tells us Manasseh burned his children in sacrifice to Molech, and 2nd Kings 21:16 tells us he filled Jerusalem with innocent blood from one end to the other. Who's blood? The blood of innocent children offered to Molech, Baal, and Ashtoreth.

Good King Josiah rose after him and tore down the pagan altars and slaughtered their priests, bringing revival and reform to Judah, but it was too little, too late. The die for judgment had been cast. 2nd Kings 24:1-4 declares:

> **1** In his days Nebuchadnezzar king of Babylon came up, and Jehoiakim became his servant for three years; then he turned and rebelled against him.
> **2** And the Lord sent against him bands of Chaldeans, bands of Arameans, bands of Moabites, and bands of Ammonites. So he sent them against Judah to destroy it, according to the word of the Lord which He had spoken through His servants the prophets.
> **3** Surely at the command of the Lord it came upon Judah, to remove them from His sight because of the sins of Manasseh, according to all that he had done,
> **4** and also for the innocent blood which he had shed, for he filled Jerusalem with innocent blood; and the Lord would not forgive.

Our God is a God of perfect justice. He takes seriously the murder of innocent human life which He created in His image, and He will judge those who wrongfully take it. God did not forget the sins of Manasseh even though he repented, and Josiah brought reform. The sword of God's perfect justice was already placed into the hand of Babylon.

America, like Jerusalem, has been filled with blood from one end to the other. We have passed through the fire over 60 million innocents offered to Molech on the altar of abortion. God did not wink at this abomination in Israel and He will certainly not let it pass in our nation, either. And yet, as we head into the presidential election cycle, it has become the main plank of the democrat platform, supported by both the godless and compromised Christians. Judgment is on its way.

Baal, Molech, and Ashtoreth want our children. If they can't slaughter them in the womb, they will enslave them after birth. To that end, we are well on our way. I am reminded of a famous narration by past popular radio host, Paul Harvey, entitled "If I Were the Devil," first broadcast April 3rd, 1965:

> "If I were the devil...I mean, if I were the Prince of Darkness, I would of course, want to engulf the whole world in darkness. I would have a third of its real estate and four-fifths of its population, but I would not be happy until I had seized the ripest apple on the tree, so I should set about however necessary to take over the United States. I would begin with a campaign of whispers. With the wisdom of a serpent, I would whisper to you as I whispered to Eve" "Do as you please." "Do as you please." To the young I would whisper, "The Bible is a myth." I would convince them that man created God instead of the other way around. I would confide that what is bad is good, and what is good is "square."

In the ears of the young marrieds, I would whisper that work is debasing, that cocktail parties are good for you. I would caution them not to be extreme in religion, in patriotism, in moral conduct. And the old, I would teach to pray. I would teach them to say after me: "Our Father, which art in Washington…"

If I were the devil, I'd educate authors in how to make lurid literature exciting so that anything else would appear dull and uninteresting. I'd threaten T.V. with dirtier movies and vice versa. And then, if I were the devil, I'd get organized. I'd infiltrate unions and urge more loafing and less work, because idle hands usually work for me. I'd peddle narcotics to whom I could. I'd sell alcohol to ladies and gentlemen of distinction. And I'd tranquilize the rest with pills. If I were the devil, I would encourage schools to refine young intellects but neglect to discipline emotions…let those run wild. I would designate an atheist to front for me before the highest courts in the land and I would get preachers to say "she's right." With flattery and promises of power, I could get the courts to rule what I construe as against God and in favor of pornography, and thus, I would evict God from the courthouse, and then from the schoolhouse, and then from the houses of Congress and then, in His own churches, I would substitute psychology for religion, and I would deify science because that way men would become smart enough to create super weapons but not wise enough to control them.

If I were Satan, I'd make the symbol of Easter, an

egg, and the symbol of Christmas, a bottle. If I were the devil, I would take from those who have and would give to those who wanted, until I had killed the incentive of the ambitious. And then, my police state would force everybody back to work. Then I could separate families, putting children in uniform, women in coal mines, and objectors in slave camps. In other words, if I were Satan, I'd just keep on doing what he's doing." [1]

Nearly six decades later, Paul Harvey's prophetic broadcast has been more than fulfilled. Through the Baals and Ashtoreths, the devil's relentless pursuit of our children continues unabated.

Today, we have pictorially pornographic books secreted into our public and school libraries with hopes no decent citizens will notice or object. In a nearby town library, new titles include: *It's Perfectly Normal; Sex is a Funny Word;* and *Let's Talk About It,* all with graphic depictions of sex available to children. Ironically, local parents who protest this literature (the taxpayers who fund the library system) are met with hostility and resistance by the library council. Ashtoreth will not be denied.

Our public schools that should be concerned solely with academics, have taken upon themselves the role of parent, teaching sexuality to our children, but from their own immoral perspective. The only thing a third-grade boy needs to know about sex is that girls have cooties, and when it comes time to teach him differently, it is done in the confines of the family. But Ishtar, using the blunt instrument of corrupt government, cudgels the public into submission through "Drag" reading sessions for children and other inappropriate programs designed to compromise them at an early age, hoping to confuse them regarding gender identity. As I write, the White House panders to this perversion, hanging a rainbow/transgender flag (a violation of all U.S. flag codes) from its balcony while the perverts dance topless below it. The President called them "brave heroes." Is this what heroism has become?

With the devil comes the diabolical. Today, the miniscule "trans" segment of our society gets way more press than it should, focusing our attention on a distraction that should never have been an issue rather than matters of serious import. The recent school shooting in Nashville serves to punctuate the anti-God bias of the transgender movement. Once again, Jonathan Cahn makes some salient points regarding this tragedy in a video he posted on YouTube. He referenced the famous story of the Geresene demoniac found in Mark 5:1-20. There the demon possessed man is seen living in the tombs which were caves in that day. The name "Hale" comes from old English which means *one who lives in nooks.* Cahn also mentioned the fact that the three adults murdered at Covenant School were all in their 60s, and the three children murdered were all 9 years of age. In demonology, the number nine is inverted. We had six people murdered, all related to the number of three sixes. [2]

The manifesto written by Audrey Hale before the murders, as of this date, has not been released. It is suspected to be a diatribe against her alma mater, Christians and Christianity. It has not been released because it does not fit the leftist narrative regarding the poor persecuted transgender community – quite the opposite. Yet, if you listened to various media outlets, it was the school's fault for the rampage, and those right-wing abusers at Covenant deserve what they got! Satan always shifts the blame.

The transgender controversy continues to fester, with WOKE businesses forcing their ideology down the throats of middle America, even at great cost to their own bottom line. Bud Light (Anheuser Busch) lost billons of dollars in profits pushing the trans message through transgendered actor, Dylan Mulvaney. Not to be outdone, Target stores opened a line of women's swimsuits tailored to be "tuck friendly" for male genitalia in its new "Pride Collection." The store lost $10 billion in market value in ten days, experiencing a 14% drop in its stock. The boycott of Target escalated when news of the company's partnership with Erik Carnell, an open transman Satanist, was chosen to design Target's "Pride Line." He was seen in a T-shirt that stated: "Satan respects pronouns. Yes, Legion, for we are many..." Target's partnership with Carnell was quickly dissolved after the $10 billion loss got their attention.

But again, Ishtar would not be denied. She simultaneously inserted herself into pro-sports when management for the Los Angeles Dodgers scheduled their own pride event in June, dis-inviting, then re-inviting the anti-God, anti-Catholic, anti-Christian Sisters of Perpetual Indulgence. What purpose these sickos had at a family event during America's favorite pastime, I cannot tell you, other than it's just another way to indoctrinate children into their evil practices.

Certainly, athletics have become the focus of weak men pretending to be women. We are now treated to mediocre male athletes, unable to compete successfully against their birth gender, exploiting women's sports for their own glory (translated "shame"). This is all done while normally outspoken feminists remain silent, and as genuine, hardworking female athletes see their hopes, dreams, aspirations and scholarships ripped away from them.

When I see clips of garish drag queens flaunting their perversion in the faces of our children, it's obvious who they are after. They openly declare as much. In the NYC pride rally held on June 24th, the chant was: "We're here, we're queer, we're coming for your kids." Unable to reproduce themselves (by the way, men can't have babies), they must recruit from the heterosexual community to perpetuate their movement. And, of course, to destroy a nation and its future, this is what you do. Satan and his right-hand devil, Ishtar, have nearly completed their mission in the U.S. Only those with spiritual eyes can see it, and only those with Holy Spirit unction will stand against it: "Therefore, to the one who knows the right thing to do, and does not do it, to him it is sin" (James 4:17).

The right thing to do in America today is to repent before God in sackcloth and ashes; to fast and pray, and declare a solemn assembly. That would be the right thing to do. But we will opt for the easy way and place our hope in one man or men, or in ourselves, or in government, not in the One True God of Heaven who is able to change the course of human history at the behest of His saints, like He did for Edwards, Frelinghuysen, Whitefield and Wesley.

Baal, Ashtoreth, and Molech have returned with a vengeance and only the power of heaven can defeat them. The Church must enlist that power.

CHAPTER 5

The Substitute God

We have just considered at length how no one and nothing, including government, can exist in a vacuum. Once the controls of government have been abandoned, others must be put in place. America's controls used to be biblical principles written into our founding documents and subsequent laws. Those are now ignored or declared "unconstitutional," being replaced with humanistic and satanic ideals. People who reject Jehovah as God substitute something else, usually self, science, and government.

A philosophy of social order was developed nearly two centuries ago when intellectual atheists in Europe decided to publish their godless beliefs. Regarding government and social order, atheists Ludwig Feuerbach (1804-1872) and Karl Marx (1818-1883) rejected religion and Christianity in particular, believing it irrelevant to the future of humanity. Marx held that the church invented religion to justify the ruling classes' exploitation of working-class labor by way of a socially stratified industrial society. He considered religion a drug that gave an emotional escape from the real world. In "A Contribution to the Critique of Hegel's Philosophy of Right," Marx described the contradictory nature of religious sentiment:

> Religious suffering is, at one and the same time, the expression of real suffering, and a protest of real suffering. Religion is the sigh of the oppressed creature, the heart of a heartless world, and the soul of soulless conditions. It [religion] is the opium of the people.[1]

German philosopher, Friedrich Engels (1820-1895), a close collaborator of Karl Marx, declared religion a fantasy and believed it would eventually disappear. Like his contemporaries, he insisted scientific advances, socio-economic and cultural progress required that atheistic materialism become a science rather than remain a philosophy apart from the sciences. In his writing, "Anti-Duhring," Engels said:

> This modern materialism, the negation of the negation, is not the mere re-establishment of the old, but adds to the permanent foundations of this old materialism the whole thought-content of two thousand years of development of philosophy and natural science, as well as of the history of these two thousand years. It [materialism] is no longer a philosophy at all, but simply a world outlook, which has to establish its validity and be applied, not in a science of sciences, standing apart, but in real sciences. Philosophy is therefore *sublated* here, that is, "both overcome and preserved"; overcome as regards its form, and preserved as regards its real content.[2]

Russian revolutionary, Vladimir Lenin, said that a true communist would always promote atheism and combat religion, because it is the psychological opiate that robs people of their human agency, of their volition, as men and women, to control their own reality. In "Socialism and Religion" (1905), Lenin said:

> Religion is one of the forms of spiritual oppression, which everywhere weighs down heavily upon the masses of the people, over-burdened by their perpetual work for others, by want and isolation. Impotence, of the exploited classes in their struggle against the exploiters, just as inevitably, gives rise to a belief in a better life after death, as [the] impotence of the savage in his battle with Nature gives rise to belief in gods, devils, miracles, and the like.
>
> Those who toil and live in want all their lives are taught, by religion, to be submissive and patient while here on earth, and to take comfort in the hope of a heavenly reward. But those who live by the labour of others are taught, by religion, to practice charity while on earth, thus offering them a very cheap way of justifying their entire existence as exploiters, and selling them, at a moderate price, tickets to well-being in heaven. Religion is opium for the people. Religion is a sort of spiritual booze, in which the slaves of capital drown their human image, their demand for a life more or less worthy of man.[3]

Scientific atheism became the philosophic basis of Marxist-Leninism, the ideology of the Communist Party in Russia, Europe, and later in several Asian nations. Vladimir Ilyich Lenin "appealed to militant atheism as a criterion for the sincerity of Marxist commitments as a testing principle."[4]

It is dizzying to read the intellectually complex gymnastics of 19th century atheists. Once again, we see the substitute idols of those who have rejected the One True God of heaven and earth, men who knew about "religion" but nothing about a personal relationship with a living Savior.

Horizontal, materialistic ideology (idolatry) based on self and so called "science," always seems to make its way into government. We saw it in Israel, we saw it in the world empires as predicted by Daniel, and we see it today. Satan will instigate, endorse and support any activity, philosophy, or religion that denies Jehovah. The denial of God and the spiritual world is, as the Marxists stated, the first step to a classless, collectivist, one-world socialist order. The capitalist systems found in scripture oppose the Marxist-Leninist economics that were imposed upon the globe during the 20th century up to the present time. The revolutions started by Lenin, Stalin, Mao and various other Eastern European and Asian communists, cost the world over 60 million lives. However, the collapse of the Soviet Union in 1991 and the failure of other communist states to deliver their promised equality and prosperity led to a decline in the popularity of communism as a political ideology. Failure to make good on economic prosperity, political freedom, and human rights led to the fall of communist governments and the rise of democratic systems in

Eastern Europe and the Soviet Union. [5] And here is the irony: Despite the failure of communism wherever it has been tried, it remains a significant influence in academic circles and in political parties of the democratic West – the United States being no exception.

Labor movements, beginning in the late 1800s, were influenced by the Socialist Labor Party and then the Socialist Party of America. After the Bolshevik Revolution in Russia, Vladimir Lenin invited the Socialist Party to join the Communist International, or COMINTERN. In the spring of 1919, the Communist Party USA (CPUSA) was founded in Chicago, Illinois. It was an active force in worker's unions, civil rights, and anti-war movements, and developed close financial ties with the Soviet Union.

During the "Red Scare" of the 1950s, the US government publicly tried and convicted Communists and CPUSA members on the grounds of the Smith Act. Then, CPUSA faced challenges when the dissolution of the Soviet Union happened and it lost its main source of funding. [6] The diminished communist organization turned its attention elsewhere, finding a welcoming host in the Democrat Party.

In 2000, Sam Webb became chairman of the Communist Party's National Committee. Under his leadership, the party's top priority became supporting the Democrats in elections in order to defeat the "ultra right." Despite the party's previous rigidity which caused a partial split, the 21st Century CPUSA was willing to align with the Democratic Party to an extent far greater than its previous internal critics had even called for. In fact, CPUSA had shifted its views to the point where they saw the 2008 election of Barack Obama as a "transformative triumph of a labor-led all peoples' movement," a far cry from previous stances. During the 2020 election CPUSA self-published articles written by party staff in tacit support of then candidate Joe Biden and in vehement opposition to President Donald Trump. CPUSA accused Trump of spreading "deadly hate" during the election. CPUSA published unofficial articles likening the 2020 election movement to install Joe Biden to another popular front. In the wake of the January 6 Capitol Riot, the party released an article calling for the forced removal of Donald Trump from office. An increasingly militant and growing youth sector played instrumental roles in the Black Lives Matter demonstrations and in the national fight to save Public Housing.[7]

Of course, CPUSA was thrilled with the election and re-election of Barack Obama. In a report by Erwin Marquit delivered to the 14th International Meeting of Communist and Worker's Parties, held in Beirut, Lebanon, November 22-25, Barack Obama was praised. Here are excerpts from Marquit's report:

> We express our gratitude to the Lebanese Communist Party for hosting this important meeting under the present difficult conditions.
>
> We believed that if the Republican candidate for President were elected and if both houses of the Congress fell under control of the far right, racist sector (calling itself the "Tea Party") that now dominates the Republican Party, the nation's return to pre-1932 conditions would be a real danger.

We are aware that some on the left in the United States thought that the correct approach to the elections was either to boycott them, or as a protest, to run or support small-scale left-wing candidacies with no possible chance of winning. We Communists rejected that strategy because too much was at stake.

The most important success of the Obama Administration since its election in 2008 was the introduction of major expansion of the people's access to financing their healthcare. As a result of this legislation, 25 million people now have access to health care who previously did not have it.

The Occupy movement, with its slogan, "We are the 99%," that swept through the country in 2011, sharply drew attention to the top 1% of the population and stimulated support for Obama's efforts to require higher taxes for the wealthy. The Republicans have blocked all proposals to reduce global warming, environment destruction, industrial pollution, and other actions arising from corporate greed and that they threaten to destroy the biophysical basis of human existence. Republicans even want to privatize the FEMA, the federal agency for disaster mitigation.

Another important issue is that of justice for immigrant workers and their families. There are between 10 and 11 million irregular immigrants in the United States, mostly from Mexico and other Latin American countries. Our party supports the regularization of their status, with full rights in the workplace and in the community, and access to U.S. citizenship. The Obama administration has moved too slowly on this issue (and the CPUSA has been sharply critical of this), but it is now taking some modest but real steps. The Republicans , on the other hand, have whipped up a racist frenzy against immigrants that has led to vigilante action and in some cases the murder of immigrant workers. Romney had promised to make life so hard for undocumented immigrants that they would all "self" deport.

Faced with a choice between the victory of either the Democratic Party or the Republican Party, the Communist Party views a victory of the far-right Republican Party as an extreme disaster.

We support immediate withdrawal of NATO troops from Afghanistan and oppose the use of drones for assassination and bombing. We call for the end of sanctions against Iran. We oppose the China-bashing policies of the U.S. government.

Reverend Gradye Parsons, the top official of the Presbyterian Church (U.S.A.) said, "We asked Congress to treat Israel like it would any other country, to make sure our military aid is going to a country espousing the values we would as Americans – that it is not being used to continually violate the human rights of other people." This is a sharp contrast to the evangelical Christian churches, which have been a part of the core of the far-right support of the Republican candidates for president and the Congress.

> A key element of the Communist Party's strategy of alliances is to imbue the struggles of these alliances with democratic rights, and to promote the increasing use of the public sector to extend the acceptance of a socialist consciousness... effectively using our participation in people's struggles and the internet to recruit new members... As a result of our on-line activities, we have been forming Party clubs in states in which we previously had very few or even no members. This influx of new members led us to have a national Party school earlier this year to acquaint new members with the Marxist-Leninist orientation of the Party.
>
> While the victory of Obama is a welcome aid for us in our domestic struggles, we still face the challenge of mobilizing mass pressure on this administration to reverse the imperialist character of U.S. foreign policy. The CPUSA will pursue the formidable task vigorously in alliance with domestic, progressive forces and with our comrades in the Communist and Worker's Parties and their allies throughout the world.[8]

Do any of Marquit's remarks look familiar? We recall the famous interaction that candidate Barack Obama had with "Joe the Plumber," explaining the higher tax bracket for those making over $250K. Obama declared: "When you spread the wealth around, it's good for everybody." No wonder he was the darling of the Communist Party, and, of course, he appointed cabinet members of the same godless ilk who remained in power long after he was term limited. Many believe Joe Biden's election was just a third term for Barack Obama with Obama on record during a Stephen Colbert interview in 2020, saying he would be perfectly comfortable with that sort of arrangement.

After suffering through the last four years of the Biden/Harris regime, it is undeniable that the implementation of the Communist agenda and the intentional destruction of the nation (couched as a "fundamental transformation") has been the goal. Co-opting by the communists has not been any more evident than in the alphabet agencies, i.e., FBI, CIA, NSA, IRS, USSS, and , sadly, the U.S. military.

In an article written by author and filmmaker G. Edward Griffin, the allegiances of FBI and CIA directors, James Comey and John Brennan, were revealed:

> The heads of Obama's FBI and CIA voted for Communists during the Cold War, yet were able to move up the ranks within the same US Intelligence community that, for decades, claimed to oppose Communism. The news media outlets missed the story when it was first published a few months ago, but it needs to be known and in the record. Former FBI Director James Comey admitted in a 2003 interview that he voted Communist before voting for Jimmy Carter in 1980. Comey added that he did not know how to classify himself politically. Former CIA Director John Brennan said that, in 1976 he voted for Gus Hall, the Communist Party candidate for President. This fact did not hinder him from becoming head of the CIA afterward [This will not be shocking

> to anyone who understands that there is no significant difference in the ideological beliefs of Communists, Fascists, Nazis, Socialists and other variants of collectivism is the dominant ideology of both major political parties today.] - G. Edward Griffin, author and filmmaker.[9]

Today, it appears Merick Garland has picked up where these men have left off, further corrupting the American intelligence agencies, making the Justice Department anything but just. Now, in hindsight, we know the Justice Department directly influenced the 2020 election in favor of the Communist candidate – withholding the damning Hunter Biden laptop and other vital information regarding Biden family corruption, not to mention coercing social media into censoring conservative viewpoints. How is that not election interference of the highest order? Certainly, it is a demonstration of contempt for both the U.S. Constitution and the American people, and highlights an evident "two-tier" justice system. Leviticus 24:22 "There shall be one standard for you; it shall be for the stranger as well as the native, for I am the Lord your God."

This is where generations of spiritual apathy and apostasy will take you. No one was minding the store when the thief came in to kill, steal, and destroy. The false gods of self and science have led us to the golden calf of government. The problem is spiritual.

David Lane in his American Renewal Project has been countering this trend for years, hoping to get Christians and Christian leaders actively engaged in the public square once again:

What is most puzzling in our own nation's setting revolves around American Christendom's surrender to secularism of America's once Judeo-Christian heritage and Biblically based culture established by the Founders. As a consequence of the Christian abandonment of the public square, spiritual worship now centers within and around the State.

The State's secular priests and priestesses banned prayer to Jehovah in public schools in 1962 [Engle v. Vitale], outlawed the Bible from public education in 1963 [Abington School District v. Schempp], miraculously discovered a constitutional "right" to kill unborn babies in 1973 [Roe v. Wade], tore down the Ten Commandments from public schools, courthouses, and government buildings in 1980 [Stone v. Graham], exalted, normalized, and codified into law homosexual intercourse and same-sex marriage in 2015 [Obergefell v. Hodges], and pronounced "special rights" for homosexuals and transgenders in 2020 [Bostock v. Clayton County].

God's enemies – Big Business, Big Tech, Bud Light, Fortune 500, and Big Biden – venerate the golden calves of multiculturalism, political correctness, and secularism as they incite instability into the culture, whip up division between races, and promote political upheaval. Deifying wokeism, Critical Race Theory, DEI [diversity, equity, inclusion], and radical environmentalism, the State's sacrosanct sacraments include abortion, "anti-racism" struggle sessions, vaccines, and obsessive recycling.

As individual freedoms wane, government mandates and edicts are now viewed as the ultimate source of authority. American Christendom meanwhile cowers behind the four walls of the church building, giving center stage to butts, buildings, and budgets instead of getting involved in the culture. Yet it would seem that a focus to ascertain God's model for cultural transformation would be deemed essential for a healthy church.

What appears certain is that very little remains of the robust theological underpinnings and inherent power [Gr. dunamis] that took off in Germany in 1517, soared in England in 1534, and began its triumphal march on the Eastern Shores of America in 1620.

What was once **publicly** declared and testified to, remains today, often even privately, unstated and unexpressed.

Famed sociologist and best-selling author Robert N. Bellah [1927-2013] spells out what it was that, after arriving at America's shores in 1620, launched America's meteoric rise in world history: *The Bible was one book that literate Americans in the 17th, 18th, and 19th centuries could be expected to know well. Biblical imagery provided the framework for imaginative thought in America up until quite recent times.*

Cunningly expunged from American culture by God's antagonists and foes, the Bible in contemporary secularized America has been largely removed from

> church houses, schoolhouses, statehouses, and courthouses so that Biblical illiteracy now monopolizes the culture.[10]

How could we have opposed godless Communism on the global stage in the hot wars of Korea and Vietnam, defeated it in the cold war with the Soviet Union, but then succumb to it ourselves? President John Adams aptly stated: "Our Constitution was made only for a moral and religious people. It is wholly inadequate to the government of any other." He also predicted in a personal letter to John Taylor written in 1814: "Democracy never lasts long. It soon wastes, exhausts and murders itself. There was never a democracy that didn't commit suicide." I suppose that is why our Christian Founders set up a Constitutional Republic and not a Democracy.

"Blessed is the nation whose God is the Lord, The people whom He has chosen for His own inheritance" (Psalm 33:12). But…

"The wicked shall be turned into hell, and all the nations that forget God" (Psalm 9:17).

CHAPTER 6

Strong Delusion

The King James Version of the Bible says in the last days, under the influence of the antichrist, God will send "strong delusion" (2nd Thessalonians2:11). I like how the Oxford Dictionary defines the term: *a false belief or judgment about external reality, held despite incontrovertible evidence to the contrary, occurring especially in mental conditions.* Similar words are: *deception, misleading, deluding, fooling, tricking, trickery, duping.* If you research the term, you will find there is actually a psychological disorder associated with it, having several subcategories, e.g., erotomania, grandiose, jealous, persecutory, somatic, and mixed.

Viewing the world today, it would appear all of mankind is under strong delusion of one kind or another. The most basic and incontrovertible truths (truth defined as "final reality") are patently denied. I tried making a partial list of the delusions we are under today, and in so doing, came up with two basic categories under which we find several kinds of delusion.

The first category pertains to God's law, i.e., His Word, which is believed can be violated without consequence, though disproven in the Garden of Eden. Here are a few delusions often seen: God does not exist; It's OK to break the Ten Commandments (idolatry, dishonoring, stealing, adultery, murder, lying, coveting); There is no hell, no devil, no heaven; You don't reap what you sow; God does not punish sin; Divorce is OK; Babies can be murdered; homosexuality and transgenderism are fine.

The second category I will call Natural or Common Sense Law which strong delusion says can also be violated without consequence. Examples: Men can be women; Men can have babies; Women can be men; Women can impregnate other women; Men can compete in women's sports as women; Women can do everything men can do; Men can do everything women can do; Humans evolved from lower life forms; Climate change is our biggest problem; Pedophilia should be legal; Spending more than you make is acceptable; Persecuting Christians and Jews is OK; Debt does not need to repaid; Covid vaccines really work; Masks prevent Covid; The border is secure; America is systemically racist; Globalization is a good thing; Crime should not be punished; The 2020 election was fraud-free; Washington D.C. is not corrupt.

The above list is by no means exhaustive but does include some of the more glaring delusions experienced today. Another term closely associated with delusion is *deception.* Satan, the great deceiver, has been deluding and deceiving man for six millennia, and without spiritual insight, one has difficulty detecting it. Consequently, his deception is usually undetected in our world today though it is rampant. All a person needs to do is go to any media outlet, all of which are controlled by the Prince of the Power of the Air (Airwaves), to find lies and intentional deception. Jesus said the devil was a liar from the beginning and the father of it (John 8:44). I guess we know who the father of most news organizations, social media, newscasters, newspapers, radio, TV, and fact checkers is. Tragically, lying has become the rule and not the exception. Worse, we have become accustomed to it. We expect to be lied to and are now comfortable with it, rarely, if ever, confronting it. Deception is the primary tool of the devil and when we lie, we are most like him. Contrast the murderer and liar of John 8:44 to the Son of God who declared: "I am the Way, and the Truth and the Life; no one comes to the Father but through Me" (John 14:6). Lies bring death. Truth brings life. But look whom the world has chosen to follow.

The Apostle Paul spoke to the Thessalonian believers about delusion and apostasy in his letter. 2nd Thessalonians 2:1-12:

> **N**ow we request you, brethren, with regard to the coming of our Lord Jesus Christ, and our gathering together to Him,
>
> **2** that you may not be quickly shaken from your composure or be disturbed either by a spirit or a message or a letter as if from us, to the effect that the day of the Lord has come.
>
> **3** Let no one in any way deceive you, for it will not come unless the apostasy comes first, and the man of lawlessness is revealed, the son of destruction,

4 who opposes and exalts himself above every so-called god or object of worship, so displaying himself as being God.
5 Do you not remember that while I was still with you, I was telling you these things?
6 And you know what restrains him now, so that in his time he may be revealed.
7 For the mystery of lawlessness is already at work; only he who now restrains will do so until he is taken out of the way.
8 And then that lawless one will be revealed whom the Lord will slay with the breath of His mouth and bring to an end by the appearance of His coming;
9 that is, the one whose coming is in accord with the activity of Satan, with all power and signs and false wonders,
10 and with all the deception of wickedness for those who perish, because they did not receive the love of the truth so as to be saved.
11 And for this reason God will send upon them a deluding influence so that they might believe what is false,
12 in order that they all may be judged who did not believe the truth, but took pleasure in wickedness.

Suffering persecution, the church at Thessalonica wondered if they had missed the Lord's return. Rumors and false messages had confused them. To eliminate the confusion, Paul gave them some markers to expect before the day of the Lord.

He said in verse 3 that: 1) apostasy – a falling away from the faith must first come, and 2) the man of lawlessness (antichrist) will be revealed. Note that these two things must occur before the "Day of the Lord" which is the time of Christ's return to judge the earth. The Day of the Lord is to be differentiated from the removal of "he who now restrains" in verse 7. The restraining one is God the Holy Spirit. He currently dwells within the heart of all true believers. We understand that when He is taken out of the way, Christians are taken up in the rapture (Gk. *harpazo* = sudden snatching away) of the church. When the restraining influence is removed, Satan's man, the antichrist, will come to power and satanic delusion on earth will be complete. However, in the meantime, John reminds us in 1st John 2:18, 22, 23:

> **18** Children, it is the last hour; and just as you heard that antichrist is coming, even now many antichrists have arisen; from this we know that it is the last hour.
> 22 Who is the liar but the one who denies that Jesus is the Christ? This is the antichrist, the one who denies the Father and the Son.
> 23 Whoever denies the Son does not have the Father; the one who confesses the Son has the Father also.

The spirit of the antichrist has been with us since the incarnation of Jesus, but that spirit has grown over the centuries and is culminating in our day. Overwhelming delusion and deception indicate such. Secularism, atheism, paganism, and false religion deny Christ and the Father. John says this is the spirit of the antichrist. Since America fell from its Christian foundation, apostasy has allowed this evil spirit to thrive. Whether it be in our families, our culture, or our government, it seems we are barely restraining it anymore. The Shining City on a Hill spoken of by Christ and referenced by Winthrop and Reagan has been greatly dimmed by sin and Satan. Its once positive global influence has been compromised, and if the present trend is not soon reversed by a major spiritual awakening, the Republic will be lost forever.

In what is known as the *Olivet Discourse,* found in Matthew chapters 24 and 25, Jesus described in detail the events that would precede His immediate return. Matthew 24:1-31:

> **A**nd Jesus came out from the temple and was going away when His disciples came up to point out the temple buildings to Him.
> 2 And He answered and said to them, "Do you not see all these things? Truly I say to you, not one stone here shall be left upon another, which will not be torn down."
> 3 And as He was sitting on the Mount of Olives, the disciples came to Him privately, saying, "Tell us, when will these things be, and what will be the sign of Your coming, and of the end of the age?"
> 4 And Jesus answered and said to them, "See to it that no one misleads you.
> 5 "For many will come in My name, saying, 'I am the Christ,' and will mislead many.

6 "And you will be hearing of wars and rumors of wars; see that you are not frightened, for those things must take place, but that is not yet the end.
7 "For nation will rise against nation, and kingdom against kingdom, and in various places there will be famines and earthquakes.
8 "But all these things are merely the beginning of birth pangs.
9 "Then they will deliver you to tribulation, and will kill you, and you will be hated by all nations on account of My name.
10 "And at that time many will fall away and will deliver up one another and hate one another.
11 "And many false prophets will arise, and will mislead many.
12 "And because lawlessness is increased, most people's love will grow cold.
13 "But the one who endures to the end, he shall be saved.
14 "And this gospel of the kingdom shall be preached in the whole world for a witness to all the nations, and then the end shall come.
15 "Therefore when you see the ABOMINATION OF DESOLATION which was spoken of through Daniel the prophet, standing in the holy place (let the reader understand),
16 then let those who are in Judea flee to the mountains;

17 let him who is on the housetop not go down to get
the things out that are in his house;
18 and let him who is in the field not turn back to get
his cloak.
19 "But woe to those who are with child and to those
who nurse babes in those days!
20 "But pray that your flight may not be in the winter,
or on the Sabbath;
21 for then there will be great tribulation, such as has
not occurred since the beginning of the world until
now, nor ever shall.
22 "And unless those days had been cut short, no life
would have been saved; but for the sake of the elect
those days shall be cut short.
23 "Then if anyone says to you, 'Behold here is the
Christ,' or 'There He is,' do not believe him.
24 "For false Christs and false prophets will arise and
will show great signs and wonders, so as to mislead, if possible, even the elect.
25 "Behold, I have told you in advance.
26 "If therefore they say to you, 'Behold, He is in the
wilderness,' do not go forth, or, 'Behold, He is in
the inner rooms,' do not believe them.
27 "For just as the lightning comes from the east, and
flashes even to the west, so shall the coming of the
Son of Man be.
28 "Wherever the corpse is, there the vultures will
gather.

> **29** "But immediately after the tribulation of those days THE SUN WILL BE DARKENED AND THE MOON WILL NOT GIVE ITS LIGHT, AND THE STARS WILL FALL from the sky, and the powers of the heavens will be shaken,
> 30 and then the sign of the Son of Man will appear in the sky, and then all the tribes of the earth will mourn, and they will see the SON OF MAN COMING ON THE CLOUDS OF THE SKY with power and great glory.
> 31 "And He will send forth His angels with A GREAT TRUMPET and THEY WILL GATHER TOGETHER HIS elect from the four winds, from one end of the sky to the other."

Like Paul, Christ gave some very concise markers that would indicate His soon coming: 1) v. 5, false Christs would arise, 2) v. 6, wars and rumors of wars, 3) v. 7, nation against nation, and kingdom against kingdom, indicating civil wars and unrest, 4) v. 7, famines and earthquakes, 5) v. 9, persecution of Christians, 6) v. 10, many will fall away in apostasy, 7) v. 11, many false prophets will arise, 8) v. 12, lawlessness will increase, 9) v. 12, people's love will grow cold and, 10) v. 14, the gospel of the kingdom shall be preached to the whole world. In his letters, the Great Apostle reiterated these ten things and included the great delusion and apostasy that would precede the Abomination of Desolation (antichrist) and Day of the Lord.

There are those who downplay, or even disbelieve in the return of Christ and, like Peter warned, will say: "Where is the promise of His coming? For ever since the fathers fell asleep, all things continue just as they were from the beginning of creation" (2nd Peter 3:4). The mockers will poo-poo God's Word and tell us throughout man's history we have always had false teachers, wars, rebellions, famines, earthquakes, and lawlessness. Certainly, we have. But Jesus qualified these things in verse 8 when he compared them to the birth pangs of a woman. Birth pangs become more intense and closer together as the birth of a child approaches. What we are seeing is earthquakes in diverse, or different places, more frequently and intensely than ever; more wars and rebellions; more famines and pestilences, and more lawlessness than ever. The birth pangs are intensifying, leading us into the Great Tribulation and the return of the Lord. By all indications "now is our salvation nearer than when we believed" (Romans 13:11).

Satan's favorite tools of deception and delusion have birthed a new era of political "gaslighting" like we have never been seen before. If you aren't familiar with the term, just know that it was Merriam-Webster's word of the year in 2022. The term originated in a 1938 British play, later made into a film, entitled *Gas Light.* The story was about a man who attempted to trick his new wife into believing she was losing her mind by telling her the gaslights in their home were not dimming, when they actually were. "Gaslight" (both adjective and noun) became a popular verb as it was actively used in psychological manipulation. Satan's godless agents use this device endlessly upon America's political stage. As I write, the propaganda machine is running non-stop, extolling the wonderful accomplishments of the Biden/Harris administration, telling us we have experienced the exact opposite of what we have experienced over the last four years. Kamala Harris now makes grandiose promises, saying she will fix all the problems - problems she and her administration caused. It's been said, those who caused the problem should not be trusted to find the solution. Yet, in a fit of satanic masochism, millions are willing to reinstall the same politicians who subjected them to abject misery over the last four years. Einstein's definition of insanity: "Doing the same thing over and over again, expecting different results."

When you see tens of thousands of illegal aliens cross our border in a single day, and President Joe Biden and Secretary of Homeland Security Alejandro Mayorkas look directly into the camera with a straight face and say, "The border is secure" – you're being gas lit. When you go to the grocery store and pay 25 to 50 percent more for food than you did 4 years ago, and they tell you, "Bidenomics is working, inflation is coming down" – you're being gas lit.

Woke military officers who infest our armed services today will tell you females are equal to males as war fighters, when study after study says otherwise. (Studies done by the U.S. Marine Corps cited in my previous book, *John Wayne, Jesus Christ and Other Faded Icons,* address this issue) We are told to disbelieve the laws of nature and physics when that which has been commonly understood since creation is denied. This same gaslighting has all but destroyed women's sports. Women are not physically equal to men in athletics. That reality is now being proven time and again by sick, pathetic, warped, unprincipled biological males who shamelessly compete against females, who then want you to believe their victories are legitimate. Another gaslight.

When, in all of human history, has anyone ever been expected to believe and accept this kind of insanity? Only now, in our modern technological age of enlightenment, declaring ourselves superior to our ancestors, do we cast off the bonds of common sense to follow nonsense, "Professing to be wise, they became fools" (Romans 1:22). Only now, under the strong biblical delusion and spiritual apostasy of these last days are we ready and willing to receive Satan's destructive agenda. The problem is spiritual.

CHAPTER 7

Betrayal

Close kin to deception is betrayal. From the beginning, betrayal has been a part of our fallen fabric. Merriam Webster defines the verb *Betray*:

> to give information about (a person, group, country, etc.) to an enemy; to hurt (someone who trusts you, such as a friend or relative) by not giving help or by doing something morally wrong; to show (something, such as a feeling or desire) without wanting or trying to. *Betrayal* is the noun form. Interestingly, Webster gives the word's etymology as coming from the Latin *tradere* – more at *traitor.*[1]

Growing up in the public education system when American history and civics were still taught, I learned of an individual named Benedict Arnold who was known for his betrayal of our country. His turning against George Washington and the American Revolution was presented as the most heinous thing a man could do. Washington thought highly of General Arnold who had performed well in battle. But a jealous and envious spirit led him to believe he had been slighted by his superior when other men received promotions he thought he deserved.

At last, an opportunity presented itself that would make things right. Appointed as commander of Fort West Point, Arnold was approached by a British agent, solicited by his Tory wife, with a bribe of 20,000 English pounds to surrender the fort. Fortunately, the plot was uncovered and the British agent hung, while Benedict Arnold switched sides and led English forces against the Continental army.

Sadly, the story of Benedict Arnold is not unique. Throughout history betrayal of trusting family, friends and nations has been common. Lucifer betrayed God's trust in pre-history as we have already seen. Then, Adam and Eve betrayed their Creator, choosing the words of Satan over the Word of God (Genesis 3). Soon after, jealousy regarding Abel's acceptable sacrifice caused brother Cain to rise up and slay him (Genesis 4). Jacob and Rebekah deceived Isaac and betrayed Esau regarding the birthright and the blessing (Genesis 27). Carrying down this generational sin, Jacob's sons betrayed their brother Joseph, selling him into slavery (Genesis 37). Delilah betrayed Samson in an illicit relationship based more on mistrust than trust (Judges 16). King Saul betrayed young David, a competent and loyal servant, whom he pursued until his death in battle with the Philistines (1st Samuel 18-26). In turn, David betrayed faithful Uriah, coveting the man's wife, having him intentionally murdered on the battlefield. For this act of treachery, the sword never departed David's household. Not long after, David's son, Absalom, led a rebellion against his father which resulted in the destruction of many in Israel (2nd Samuel 13-19).

Ultimately, the greatest betrayal of all time was done to the only begotten Son of God, Jesus Christ. Like Benedict Arnold, who should have taken a lesson from scripture, the name Judas Iscariot is synonymous with betrayal. His motivations are not completely clear, other than he was greedy and stole from the common purse. He sold his Lord for 30 pieces of silver, the price of a slave, betraying Him with a kiss (Luke 22). It appears greed is one way the devil can get to us, for John 13:27 says: "After the morsel, Satan then entered into him. Therefore Jesus said to him, 'What you do, do quickly.'" Of course, this act was known from all eternity past and the Psalmist wrote of it 1000 years before Christ was crucified in Psalm 41:9: "Even My close friend in whom I trusted, Who ate my bread, Has lifted up his heel against me." And during His public ministry, Jesus, referencing the Psalmist, declared: "The Son of Man is to go, just as it is written of Him; but woe to that man by whom the Son of Man is betrayed! It would have been good for that man if he had not been born" (Matthew 26:24) – chilling words from the Savior.

From the crucifixion story, we learn that it was not just Judas Iscariot who betrayed Christ. Scripture shows us He was given up by the entire nation, a sad theme continually repeated in Israel's long relationship with Jehovah.

When we read the writings of Moses and his record of the exodus from Egypt, we are struck by the nation's pre-disposition to idolatry. Beginning with the golden calf set up by Aaron in the wilderness, God's chosen people quickly resorted to idols any time the going got tough - despite miracle after miracle from God that they had seen with their own eyes. The familiar adage: *seeing is believing*, certainly was not true in Israel. In fact, according to Romans 10:17, it is not seeing but hearing that causes belief: "faith comes by hearing and hearing by the Word of God."

Proverbs 6:16-19 lists seven things the Lord hates, but even beyond that list, God hates the sin of idolatry more. In fact, its prohibition was fully established in the first two commandments of the Decalogue. No wonder Moses smashed the stone tablets when he descended the mountain and found the nation had literally broken all ten commandments during his absence. Yet, the great judgment that followed still did not stop the people from murmuring and complaining against God on their sojourn to the Promised Land. Nor did they abandon the idolatry they had learned in Egypt.

Numbers 14 records the betrayal of the spies who brought back a bad report about the land Jehovah had intended to give Israel. Their negative influence on the people brought a judgment that would condemn them to wander the wilderness for 40 years. Eventually, after the demise of that rebellious generation, Joshua was able to begin the conquest of Canaan. But Israel was never able to fully eradicate the pagan Canaanites as the Lord had commanded, and their idolatrous practices became a snare (Deuteronomy 7:16, 25; 12:30). The very thing God warned them about came to pass. By the end of King Solomon's reign, idol worship had once again made its way into Israel. Soon thereafter the kingdom split and the ten northern tribes returned to golden calf worship under the direction of Jeroboam.

By 722 BC, the Lord had had enough of Israel's spiritual betrayal. They were conquered by Assyria and deported. Judah did not learn the lesson of her sister and went even deeper into idolatry. Speaking to His people through the prophets, the Lord equated spiritual infidelity to marital infidelity. In His message to Judah and Jerusalem through the prophet Ezekiel, God used very explicit terms to describe their betrayal of His spiritual trust. The figures of betrothal and marriage and the intimacy of a husband and wife are compared to the spiritual intimacy Jehovah had with His chosen Israel.

Ezekiel's ministry was primarily to the Jewish captives in Babylon. His theme was "that they know Jehovah is Lord." In chapter 16, an abandoned infant (Jerusalem) becomes a beautiful young woman wedded to the Lord seen in Ezekiel 16:

> **8** "Then I passed by you and saw you, and behold, you were at the time for love: so I spread my skirt over you and covered your nakedness, I also swore to you and entered into a covenant with you so that you became Mine," declares the Lord God.
>
> 14 "Then your fame went forth among the nations on account of your beauty, for it was perfect because of My splendor which I bestowed on you," declares the Lord God.
>
> **15** "But you trusted in your beauty and played the harlot because of your fame, and you poured out your harlotries on every passer-by who might be willing..."

Judah's spiritual adultery with the fertility cults produced physical children who were offered in sacrifice to the pagan gods.

> 20 "Moreover, you took your sons and daughters whom you had borne to Me and sacrificed them to idols to be devoured. Were your harlotries so small a matter?
> 21 "You slaughtered My children and offered them up to idols by causing them to pass through the fire..."

In chapter 23, God gave Ezekiel another allegory regarding both the Northern and Southern Kingdoms. The two sisters, Oholah and Oholibah (Israel/Samaria and Judah/Jerusalem) are described as lustful harlots both spiritually and politically. The first eleven verses speak of Oholah's (Northern Kingdom's) whoredom with Assyria and how God handed her over to that empire for judgment. Verses 12-35 speak to the adultery of Oholibah (Southern Kingdom) and how she exceeded her sister in lewdness. Reading this chapter, you will understand why most Bible teachers avoid teaching the book of Ezekiel in worship or Sunday School. When I taught through it in men's bible study at my home, even some of them were embarrassed to read the sexually explicit language given by God to the prophet. Yet, this device highlights the gravity of spiritual unfaithfulness by a people whom God has chosen as His own. The Lord views it as the worst of all betrayals due to the damage it causes spiritually, materially, and eternally.

All material things have a spiritual connection. We find in our world, as seen in the Bible, political betrayal happens due to spiritual failure. A severe lack of spiritual discernment by a majority of Americans has allowed Satan to run his game almost unopposed. Either by vote or by fraud, the citizens of this once great land have allowed the barbarians through the gates. Deceivers and betrayers are taking down this nation at an alarming rate.

In Joshua 9, we find a story that has application to the current deception and betrayal of the U.S. There we see the inhabitants of Gibeon, aware of God's command to destroy all the inhabitants of Canaan, plot to deceive Israel. Approaching Joshua's camp at Gilgal, they feigned to be stangers from far away, seeking a truce with God's people. They even had worn out clothing and moldy bread to prove it! Eventually, their subterfuge was discovered, but not before Joshua and the nation had made an irrevocable covenant to do them no harm. The Gibeonite deception allowed them to remain in the midst of the land, albeit as perpetual slaves. Yet, their masquerade is not unlike the betrayers of America who dwell in our midst today. We don't have to go far to find them.

What about the criminal betrayal by the CDC and FDA along with the World Health Organization during the scamdemic? What about Big Media, Big Tech, and Big Government that got even bigger because of this betrayal? And likely the biggest beneficiary of all of this was Big Pharma who betrayed – and is betraying – the American people, peddling their poisons for obscene profit under the banner of good health. Satan's henchmen, indeed.

Then there was the betrayal by the teacher's unions of our youth, who not only lost years of education, but lost opportunities for scholarships and advancement in life, not to mention the loss of physical health, not by COVID but by poisonous forced inoculations.

How about the military? What about the young patriots who enlisted to protect their country only to be betrayed by corrupt leaders who summarily discharged them for refusing to be poisoned? At this moment, the same woke military is begging them to return because of abysmal recruitment numbers as we teeter on the brink of World War III. Let me say from experience, no MAN wants to serve with an outfit whose priorities are pronouns, gay pride, and transgenderism! The current woke military and corrupt U.S. government have effectively neutralized our armed forces and spit on the sacrifice of every true serviceman and patriot that has gone before.

For months now we have watched the ongoing lawfare and betrayal by the (In)Justice Department in its ongoing persecution of former President Donald Trump. Blatant bogus, unconstitutional, and irrelevant charges have been brought against the man by bought and paid for district attorneys of the America hater, George Soros. This overt commission of injustice is only eclipsed by the Department's overt omission of justice for the Biden crime family, all done in the face of overwhelming evidence of bribery and corruption.

As I write, Israel is at war with Islamic terrorism sponsored by Iran. America has always stood with the Jewish people and the State of Israel. But over these last decades a spirit of antisemitism has crept into our land. Promoted by the leftist institutions of "higher education" (i.e., indoctrination) and Muslim influencers, two generations of young Americans have been turned against an important segment of our society. I am personally appalled by the riots and demonstrations allowed on our streets and college campuses, and the attacks on Jewish citizens and students. I am amazed that we have so many Islamic sympathizers in our government who hate both Israel and the United States, who wasted no time demonstrating support for Hamas and Hezbollah while condemning Israel. And each time I witness this satanic opposition to God's chosen people, I shudder, expecting the Lord's certain wrath at any moment. For His covenant promise to Abraham, Isaac, and Jacob has never been revoked "I will bless those who bless you, and the one who curses you I will curse" (Genesis 12:3).

At this time the U.S. is condemning its only Middle East ally, Israel, for kicking UNRWA out of the Gaza territory after finding that its so-called relief workers participated in the October 7, 2023 attack. Israel is being wrongly accused of starving Palestinians when it is Hamas that confiscates relief supplies from its own people. Consequently, the current anti-Israel democrat administration is withholding vital war material from the Jewish nation as they fight for their life. Our godless leadership is literally bringing Jehovah's curse down upon us by cursing Israel in this way. The present distress in which we find ourselves will only compound as we turn our backs on God's chosen people; if we fail to "pray for the peace of Jerusalem" as Psalm 122:6 commands. God will not look kindly upon the U.S. if we go the way of every previous empire that cursed the Jew, those empires who now find themselves upon the ash heap of history.

1st Timothy 6:10 tells us the love of money is the root of all sorts of evil. Another betrayal based upon this illicit love affair has turned American executives against their own country. The promise of massive personal profit at the expense of America's national security does not phase them a bit. This is true of an untold number of U.S. politicians as well. The seduction of cheap (slave) labor that lowers production costs has caused the greed driven to look away from the human misery involved, while political leaders compromise American sovereignty and security with an adversary whose goal is to supplant us. The sale of U.S. real estate to China and other foreign nations betrays federal law but follows the pattern of controlled demolition taken from the Marxist playbook.

Opening our borders to international lawbreakers (because if you cross our borders illegally, you are a lawbreaker) and terrorists is a betrayal of bona fide citizens government is charged to protect. But when you are considered "nazi garbage" as democrat leadership calls us, don't expect your interests to be a priority. In the last four years, millions of illegals have poured over our borders unabated, many flown directly into our interior on government aircraft. Indeed, they are aided and abetted with free cell phones, gift cards, voter IDs, luxury hotels, free medical (including sex change), and a free ride to any place in the U.S. they wish to go. As a result, the whole world has flocked to our shores. Foreign governments have emptied their prisons and mental institutions and shipped their home-grown criminals to us. Accordingly, we are now experiencing an unprecedented rise in alien violent crime.

This treasonous betrayal continues as government devalues America's currency along with the value of our labor. At this writing, printing presses are rolling and the U.S. dollar becomes more worthless by the day. BRICS, an acronym for Brazil, Russia, India, China, and South Africa, a coalition of emerging market countries created by Goldman Sachs, was supposed to dominate the world economy by 2050. This group has made overtures to other nations with one goal being the replacement the U.S. dollar as the world's reserve currency. I consider this an extremely dangerous prospect as the current administration consigns our nation to unprecedented inflation.

The popular and overused term today is "existential threat." Certainly, the things mentioned so far are exactly that, but as stated early and often in previous chapters, the existential is birthed from the spiritual. America has been on Satan's "to do" list for some 300 years. It now appears he has enough inside help to finally accomplish his mission. Americans are slow to acknowledge that government is not their friend. Most refuse to believe it is as nefarious as it is, failing to realize satanic principalities and powers and spiritual wickedness in high places now rule. Our obvious lack of spiritual discernment due to Christian apostasy has opened the gates to the ancient pagan gods of history now rushing into the gap, and we are too blind to see it.

CHAPTER 8

Judgment

The great evangelist, Billy Graham, often declared that if God did not judge America, He owed Sodom and Gomorrah an apology. Many believe America is too good to receive God's judgment, but I would submit that judgment isn't coming to America, judgment is already here! The Old Testament prophets show us God did not hold back judgment, even from His chosen people, Israel, when they became unfaithful and fell into apostasy and idolatry. Indeed, He brought the severest form of judgment against them, using sword, famine, pestilence and wild animals to exact His perfect justice.

Israel's cycle of faith, to apostasy, to judgment, to repentance, back to faith, was oft repeated over the centuries of her existence. Each time the nation fell away into sin, it was judged. Romans 11:20, 21 "...Do not be conceited, but fear; for if God did not spare the natural branches, He will not spare you either." What makes us believe we here in the good ol' USA are exempt – we who have been blessed of God more than any other nation on earth? We who have had an even greater light than Israel through the Christ of Christianity? Luke 12:47, 48 "And that slave who knew his master's will and did not get ready or act in accord with his will, will receive many lashes… From everyone who has been given much, much will be required; and to whom they entrusted much, of him they will ask all the more."

Can anyone look at America's present situation and honestly believe that God is pleased with our behavior? Indeed, it seems like the dam has broken and the torrents of God's wrath are crashing down upon us. But it takes spiritual eyes to see it. All the problems we are experiencing today were the same ones experienced by Israel when she abandoned the Lord.

Polls say the biggest issue facing Americans today is inflation. Every single person in the land is affected by it. The federal government's obscene spending of taxpayer dollars has buried us beneath a mound of debt from which we can never emerge. Typically, during an inflation cycle, wages stagnate while costs rise. Today's average family must now take in an additional $12,000.00 annually to maintain the lifestyle it had four years ago. The government has proven itself expert at wasting your money. Why not? After all, it's *your* money, not theirs. The legalized theft called "taxation" is never ending. It is one of two sure things – death being the other. And sadly, the money is not used for the benefit of those from whom it has been extorted. The recent failure of FEMA to aid the citizens of North Carolina after hurricane Helene is a prime example. The Federal Emergency Management Agency's priorities were found to be aiding illegal aliens, not bona fide U.S. citizens, while ruined homes displaying Trump election materials were intentionally skipped over.

In the last several years a huge shift in wealth has occurred as Marxist politicians send your dollars to every country on the globe for reasons that make no sense to us. At present, a pet project of the compromised ruling class is the Ukraine. Long known for money laundering and corruption, the Ukraine has serviced the Biden family and others with your tax dollars. It has become a regular thing for the president of the Ukraine to visit America for his scheduled shakedown of our politicians, extracting additional billions every time he arrives. This is just one of the more publicly known boondoggles.

It seems we are playing the harlot with a majority of the nations around the globe, not unlike Jerusalem of Ezekiel 16:30-34:

> **30** "How languishing is your heart," declares the Lord God, "while you do all these things, the actions of a bold-faced harlot.
>
> 31 "When you built your shrine at the beginning of every street and made your high place in every square, in disdaining money, you were not like a harlot.
>
> 32 "You adulterous wife, who takes strangers instead of her husband!
>
> 33 "Men give gifts to all harlots, but you give your gifts to all your lovers to bribe them to come to you from every direction for your harlotries.
>
> 34 "Thus you are different from those women in your harlotries, in that no one plays the harlot as you do, because you give money and no money is given you; thus you are different."

Political and spiritual harlotry was the sin of Israel and Judah that brought judgment. They paid for alliances with pagan nations instead of relying on the Lord, importing their idolatry. They were compared to a prostitute who pays her lovers, instead of the other way around: "Because you have not remembered the days of your youth but have enraged Me by all these things, behold, I in turn will bring your conduct down on your own head," declares the Lord God, "so that you will not commit this lewdness on top of all your other abominations" (Ezekiel 16:43). Because we have used our financial blessing given by God to commit acts of political and spiritual whoredom, we will suffer the same judgment as Judah. Meanwhile, American citizens struggle to meet ends with mounting credit card debt, now placing us over one trillion in the red on plastic. Truly, the judgment of inflation is killing our economy like it did in unfaithful Israel of Haggai's day. Haggai 1:5-11:

> 5 Now therefore, thus says the Lord of hosts, "Consider your ways!
>
> 6 "You have sown much, but harvested little; you eat but there is not enough to be satisfied; you drink, but there is not enough to become drunk; you put on clothing, but no one is warm enough; and he who earns, earns wages to put into a purse with holes."
>
> 7 Thus says the Lord of hosts, "Consider your ways!
>
> 8 "Go up to the mountains, bring wood and rebuild the temple, that I may be pleased with it and be glorified," says the Lord.

9 "You look for much, but behold, it comes to little; when you bring it home, I blow it away. Why?" declares the Lord of hosts, "Because of My house which lies desolate, while each of you runs to his own house.

10 "Therefore, because of you the sky has withheld its dew and the earth has withheld its produce.

11 "I called for a drought on the land, on the mountains, on the grain, on the new wine, on the oil, on what the ground produces, on men, on cattle, and on all the labor of your hands."

Do you see how closely connected spiritual failure is to financial failure? God's material blessing upon Israel was directly related to their worship of Him. When the returned exiles complacently neglected His mandate to rebuild the temple (thus, their spiritual life), He withheld His blessing. In fact, He thwarted the efforts of their labor. The problem of inflation and bad economies is spiritual. Man-made solutions will not overcome God's judgment in the matter. The book of Deuteronomy, chapter 28, is an emphatic declaration by the Lord how He would materially bless Israel when they were faithful, and how He would materially curse them when they were disobedient. A spiritual awakening in America would go a long way toward tamping down runaway inflation and personal debt in this country.

It is obvious poor economics are a result of poor policies – intentionally poor it seems. Elected (supposedly) representatives we send to congress are to represent our interests in the laws and decisions they make. How represented have you felt lately? Did you authorize spending in the Ukraine? Or the UN? Or Iran? Or to other foreign enemies? Did you authorize the daily overwhelming influx of illegal aliens crashing our borders and financial aid to move them to our interior with gift cards, cell phones, and expensive 5-star hotels? Oh, and don't forget tax dollars for transgender surgery if they want it. We can't take care of our homeless veterans out on the streets, but we have plenty of money to care for the criminal alien army now occupying our land.

Invasion was a judgment God used against Israel. He is using it against us today. The intentionally treasonous policies of the Biden/Harris administration are meant to diminish America's strength and sovereignty and to keep the left in perpetual power. Obama's Marxist philosophy of "spreading the wealth" endorsed by the Biden regime has done a pretty thorough job of mitigating both our identity and our freedom.

Bad leadership is another judgment of God. Isaiah 3:4, 5:

> 4 And I will make mere lads their princes, And capricious children will rule over them,
> 5 And the people will be oppressed, Each one by another, and each one by his neighbor; The youth will storm against the elder And the inferior against the honorable.

I like an axiom I heard recently: "Hard times create hard men; hard men create good times; good times create soft men; soft men create hard times." And round and round it goes in parallel to Jewish history and the Tytler Cycle. America's leadership is not only soft, but villainous, just like the leadership of Rome before it fell. Again, the Lord heaped condemnation upon the leaders of Israel who proved to be false shepherds of the people. Prophets, priests, elders, and kings all had their own self-interests at heart. Ezekiel 34:1-4:

> **1** Then the word of the Lord came to me saying,
> 2 "Son of man prophesy against the shepherds of Israel. Prophesy and say to those shepherds, 'Thus says the Lord God, "Woe, shepherds of Israel who have been feeding themselves! Should not the shepherds feed the flock?
> 3 "You eat the fat and clothe yourselves with the wool, you slaughter the fat sheep without feeding the flock.
> 4 "Those who are sickly you have not strengthened, the diseased you have not healed, the broken you have not bound up, the scattered you have not brought back, nor have you sought for the lost; but with force and with severity you have dominated them."

We have 535 federal legislators between the House and the Senate; a President and Vice-President, and 9 Supreme Court justices that comprise the three branches of federal government. That totals 546 individuals. I asked the men at Bible study the other night how many people in total they thought might be in American government, including state and local.

The agreed upon number was somewhere around 4000. Of course, that did not include petty pork barrel bureaucracies, overgrown cabinets, frivolous federal departments, or the woke military. But if you look at legal, legitimate and constitutional offices only, you may have a total of 5000? Say double – 10,000? Say triple – 15,000? So, using the highest estimate of legitimate office holders, we have 15K (OK, say 20,000) leading, *ruling and dictating* to a population of 330 million! Notice, I did not say "representing" or "serving." I am amazed that 330 million people are so easily cowed by so few. I am amazed that 330 million citizens will submit to lockdowns, mandates, business closures, and forced inoculations by so few; amazed that we let the godless narrative of race and gender be set by such a small minority; amazed we tolerate the lawless, criminal and immoral behavior by these few to be done with our hard-earned taxpayer dollars. Truly, the judgment of Isaiah 3:4 is here, "capricious children" are ruling over us.

It seems the "mere lads" and "capricious children" of America have found similar playmates around the globe. Our false shepherds, mere lads, and capricious children have agreed to play the globalist game together at the direction of their head coach, Satan. But the devil's game is not a friendly competition, his game is for eternal keeps. He doesn't want just a third world country here, or an industrialized nation there. He wants the whole nine yards. He wants the whole world and has found many useful idiots willing to help him get it.

The World Economic Forum held its 54th annual meeting in Davos, Switzerland last January. Global elitists flew in on their multi-million dollar, fuel guzzling, polluting, private jets to discuss how they can make you conform to their climate change agenda. The opening ceremony (Prayer?) was conducted by a pagan witch.

During the conference, they discussed ways to reduce the earth's population so there will be more planet for them. They made unilateral decisions about who should live and who should die as they exercised their godlike prerogatives. In order for their satanically inspired plans to come together, they decided there can be no strong nationally minded U.S. standing in their way, inhibiting "one world" unity and compliance. America must be compromised economically, socially, culturally, and spiritually if the devil's plan is going to work. As we witness the collapse of our once revered institutions, it seems it is "go time" for the WEF. And when God finally pulls the trigger on the rapture, Satan's man will immediately take center stage. Satan's messiah will cement the world economically, politically, and religiously. According to Daniel 8:25 "...he shall magnify himself in his heart, and by peace shall destroy many: he shall also stand up against the Prince of princes; but he shall be broken without hand" (KJV).

One thing the WEF hopes to accomplish in the near future is the adoption of a global currency. But as long as the U.S. dollar remains the world's premier reserve currency, that cannot happen. Expect our own political traitor's help in engineering the downfall of the dollar. This will work right into antichrist's perfect plan for global economic control. A cashless world will bring us directly to Revelation 13:17 "...and he provides that no one will be able to buy or sell, except the one who has the mark, either the name of the beast or the number of his name."

We have all experienced tightening bank regulations in our personal finance. Things that should not concern the government have become government's concern. The amount of money you make and how you spend it is now of federal interest. And as big brother peers over your shoulder, he observes what you own and how he can control both it and you. A worldwide digital currency will make his work so much easier when he can monitor the credits in your account rather than the cash in your wallet. It already works this way in communist China. Research is now being done on how you can be "debanked."

As most of the planet worships and serves the god of mammon, it should come as no surprise that the Lord will eventually judge this idol. It appears this judgment is getting underway and will be connected to the predicted coming famines.

As I write, war between Israel, Hamas, Hezbollah and Iran rages. The Ukraine/Russian war slogs on and we continue to get ourselves deeper into each one. The early fear of wider regional conflict has now morphed into fear of World War III because godless, weak U.S. leadership made us militarily vulnerable on the global stage.

The 20th Century was christened "The Century of Warfare," but this century will out distance it if we remain on the current trajectory. Jesus predicted wars and rumors of wars as a sign of the last days just before His return, likening it and other signs to the birth pangs of a woman (Matthew 24; Luke 21). As we know, before a baby is born, birth pangs, i.e., contractions become more intense and closer together. The signs of false prophets, false Christs, nation against nation, lawlessness, and famines and earthquakes, will all greatly intensify right before Jesus comes back (Matthew 24:1-14). It looks like we are there.

Given the dramatic rise of global antisemitism and the escalation of hatred and warfare against Israel, it seems the contractions are becoming more frequent and intense with no hope of letting up. Regarding this conflict and the foolish war in the Ukraine, many have stated we are already at the start of World War III. I am concerned that the U.S. remain staunchly committed to Israel that we may not fall under the curse of Genesis 12:3. We are now facing serious military challenges in Europe, the Middle East and Asia as well.

Communist China's long held plans for Taiwan are coming closer to fruition. The apparent wokeness (spelled w-e-a-k-n-e-s-s) of our military has done nothing but encourage the CCP, Russia, Iran, and North Korea to move forward with their expansionism. The past successful philosophies of "peace through strength" and "speak softly and carry a big stick; you will go far" have been abandoned for a kinder, gentler, feminine military that has forgotten its mission and how to produce warriors able to defend the Constitution of the United States against all enemies foreign and domestic. God will use a sword on apostate America just as He did on Israel and Judah, and there will be no defense.

Not only does the Lord use sword and famine to judge a wayward people, but pestilence and wild animals are at His disposal as well. We are reminded of the ten plagues of Egypt that eventually released the Hebrews from captivity. If you study the different pestilences Moses unleashed upon the Egyptians, you will find that each was a direct assault upon a false deity of the pagans. Likewise, the judgments God has brought and shall bring to the U.S. will be against our own false deities.

In 2019 a largely unknown pestilence was released upon the world by none other than the CCP. What a surprise. Sadly, American dollars were actually responsible for the development and release of a Covid virus that killed millions on the earth and placed more power into the hands of our enemies both locally and abroad. It worked quite well in perpetuating the election fraud that gave us Marxist majorities in state, federal, and local elections. Unconstitutional mail-in voting, ballot harvesting, ballot forgery, unverified registrations, and voting machine inversions, were excused because of the so called "pandemic." It worked very well for Satan's power-hungry minions who gleefully snatched the levers of government away from those to whom they rightfully belonged.

At this writing we are into the 2024 election cycle and are hearing warnings about a new virus dubbed *Disease X*. Perhaps it will be here just in time for the election. Why not? After all, it worked so well the first time around. October surprise? I saw an apt cartoon using the famous painting by Howard Chandler Christy of George Washington on the platform at the signing of the U.S. Constitution. His words to the delegates were dubbed: "None of this counts if people get sick, right?" Unfortunately, the satire proved accurate. Now, with our porous border, the nation sustains all manner of disease walking in from around the world. Childhood maladies like measles, once considered all but eradicated in the U.S., are springing up again. Cases of tuberculosis as well as ancient diseases like bubonic plague, and leprosy are being seen – and that's in the illegals we know about. Who knows what the "got-aways" are carrying (other than fentanyl)! But once again, what a perfect opportunity for Big Pharma and Big Government to collude. Lockdowns and fraudulent elections will keep the godless in power while forced inoculations and fake vaccines keep pharma in profit.

In Leviticus 26 the Lord warned Israel of the judgments He would bring if they deviated from His statutes. The writer lists all that we have spoken of so far, and then adds: "I will let loose among you the beasts of the field, which will bereave you of your children and destroy your cattle and reduce your number so that your roads lie deserted" (Leviticus 26:22). Jeremiah reiterated: "Therefore the lion from the forest will slay them, A wolf of the deserts will destroy them, A leopard is watching their cities. Everyone who goes out from them will be torn in pieces, Because their transgressions are many, Their apostasies are numerous" (Jeremiah 5:6). In the last book of the New Testament, John shows us the judgments of God never change: "I looked, and behold, an ashen horse; and he who sat on it had the name Death; and Hades was following with him. Authority was given to them over a fourth of the earth, to kill with sword, and with famine and with pestilence and by the wild beasts of the earth" (Revelation 6:8).

Naïve wildlife management done by legislators and lawyers downtown rather than conservationists, outdoorsmen, ranchers and farmers on the land, has produced an unhealthy imbalance in animal populations. Tree huggers who swear that "animals are people, too" have negatively influenced decisions by natural resource departments across the states. The re-introduction of predators such as the grey wolf has decimated elk herds in the west along with domestic cattle. In the Upper Peninsula of Michigan, where the once eradicated wolf has been brought back, a previously abundant whitetail population has been reduced to a token. The situation has actually become dangerous for local residents, their pets and livestock. Ruffed Grouse hunters that I know have had prize bird dogs slaughtered and devoured by these huge pack predators.

Here in Michigan the black bear population has also grown significantly, moving farther and farther south in its range. Coyotes have increased exponentially, a predator that was all but unheard of when I was a youth. Recently, mountain lions (not bobcats) have been seen in the state, frequently captured on private game cameras. Again, something unheard of in my younger years, but can and will become a judgment of the nation if the Lord so chooses. In fact, He did choose to use them against apostate Israel recorded by the prophets.

Certainly, America will not escape God's wrath, as we have not only trespassed against the statutes of the Lord, but we have abused His mercy and His grace. We have tested the Lord our God and pushed beyond His longsuffering patience: "Be not deceived, God is not mocked, for whatsoever a man [or nation] soweth, that shall he also reap" (Galatians 6:7 KJV). Because, when you sow to the wind, you reap the whirlwind (Hosea 8:7). And friends, the gales are blowing!

CHAPTER 9

Our Hope and Remedy

We have established that war is spiritual, and spiritual conflicts must be fought with spiritual weapons (2nd Corinthians 10:4). One of my peeves with the church in general is its unbiblical view regarding philosophy of purpose. Most might agree that the Great Commission (Matthew 18:19, 20) and the Great Commandment (Matthew 22:32, 39) are duties of this New Testament institution. Yet, the philosophy of what *church* really is varies greatly between assemblies. Some view the church as an exclusive fraternity where only elites are allowed membership, or a country club to be visited at leisure for leisure. Some look at the church as a hospital where the emotionally injured are tended. Others view it as a social welfare agency whose purpose is the distribution of goods and services. Most have the idea that *church* is a building that stands on the corner. But few picture the church on earth the way Jesus and the apostles described it.

Christ told His disciples He would build His church (EKKLESIA), and the gates of hell would not prevail against it (Matthew 16:18). The terms *ekklesia* in Greek, and *ecclesia* in Latin mean both a particular body of faithful people, and the whole body of the faithful. The word is a compound of two segments: *ek*, a preposition meaning *out of*, and a verb *kaleo*, signifying *to call out*. That usage soon disappeared and was replaced with *assembly*, *congregation*, *council*, or *convocation*. [1] Using this term in the context of Matthew's gospel, we recognize it as more than just a *called-out assembly*. What we actually see here is an army – a military organization storming the strongholds of iniquity. Certainly, there is a wide variety of names for Christ's church in the Bible, e.g., the body of Christ, the bride of Christ, city of the living God, flock of God, golden candlestick, God's building, the habitation of God, the house of God, the temple of God, etc., etc. But most of these names are more descriptive of its likeness than of its activity and mission.

The Christian church in its missional work has been referred to as *The Church Militant,* a title more often employed by Catholics than evangelicals. The name places emphasis on the struggles of the church in all ages to advance the kingdom of God and defeat the kingdom of Satan. This perspective was the one carried to the New World by our founders during its earliest settlement. It certainly was the perspective of Christ and the Apostle Paul.

In his letters, Paul frequently used military metaphors to describe the church and its work. Ephesians 6:12-17:

> 12 For our struggle is not against flesh and blood, but against the rulers, against the powers, against the world forces of this darkness, against the spiritual forces of wickedness in the heavenly places.

13 Therefore, take up the full armor of God, so that you will be able to resist in the evil day, and having done everything, to stand firm.
14 Stand firm therefore, HAVING GIRDED YOUR LOINS WITH TRUTH, and HAVING PUT ON THE BREASTPLATE OF RIGHTEOUSNESS,
15 and having shod YOUR FEET WITH THE PREPARTAION OF THE GOSPEL OF PEACE;
16 in addition to all, taking up the shield of faith with which you will be able to extinguish all the flaming arrows of the evil one.
17 And take THE HELMET OF SALVATION, and the sword of the Spirit, which is the word of God.

In Ephesians 6, Paul goes into great detail describing the battle regalia the individual Christian is to don for combat against spiritual wickedness in high places. He also exhorted Pastor Timothy to: "Fight the good fight of faith" (1st Timothy 6:12) and to, "suffer hardship with me as a good soldier of Jesus Christ" (2nd Timothy 2:3, 4) and, to the Corinthians declared, "...by the weapons of righteousness for the right hand and the left" (2nd Corinthians 6:7).

The earth is a battlefield upon which the church of Jesus Christ is to be engaged, using the weapons of spiritual warfare. The problem, as seen earlier, is that the church either does not know it is in a spiritual battle, or intentionally refuses to acknowledge the fact. But it will take a correct view of the church and its calling, and a willingness to obey, before it can successfully accomplish the mission its Commander in Chief has assigned it.

Evidence of our ancestor's belief in the Church Militant was reflected, not only in their lives and conduct, but in their worship and music. Each time I attend a contemporary service today, I lament the lost worship heritage of the past. A couple of generations have grown up now without the benefit of the doctrine and inspiration of the old hymns. Certainly, not all of them were great, but it seems we have thrown the proverbial baby out with the bathwater.

If you researched (or grew up with) what used to be Sunday morning fare, you would be amazed at the number of musical scores that have been relegated to the ash heap of apostasy. The concept of the Christian church acting like an army, storming the gates of hell, is foreign to the contemporary, complacent church today. Listening to unsingable melodies and self-focused lyrics, will give you a pretty good idea of a church's philosophy of ministry. If you hear just one traditional hymn in an evangelical service (which is not too much to ask), it would be surprising. Yet, it could have the effect of blessing those over age 60, and teach valuable lessons to those under it.

The philosophy of ministry of the average non-traditional, non-mainline local assembly does not relate to The Church Militant or its music. If you go on-line to a web site called *hymntime.com*, and pull up the subtitle *spiritual warfare*, you will find a list of 295 old hymns with titles you've never heard before, such as: *Army of the Lord, The Battle Song of the Church, Forward Soldiers, Glorious Army, I Am a Little Soldier,*

March Onward, Mission War Song, Soldiers of Christ Arise!, Volunteers to the Front, Who Is On the Lord's Side, etc. [2] There are at least three which come to mind that should be a little familiar: *Battle Hymn of the Republic, Stand Up, Stand Up for Jesus* and, *Onward Christian Soldiers.* Each has an interesting back story.

Words to the *Battle Hymn of the Republic* were penned by a woman named Julia Ward Howe (1819 – 1910). In November of 1861 she and her husband visited Washington D.C. While there, Howe, a published poet, heard Union troops belting out a well-known marching song titled *John Brown's Body,* after the famously executed abolitionist, John Brown. A preacher, standing with Howe, suggested she write new lyrics to the tune. Howe later wrote: "I awoke the next morning in the gray of the early dawn... something of importance had happened to me." That "something of importance" proved to be the words to the *Battle Hymn of the Republic.* The new song spread quickly throughout the Union army and was adopted by Union supporters who wanted to teach the Southern rebels a lesson. [3] Howe's lyrics were inspired by and taken from scripture – primarily the book of Revelation.

Another hymn inspired by Paul's exhortation "to stand," seen in Ephesians 6, is *Stand Up, Stand Up for Jesus.* In the midst of the "Great Work of God" that took place in Philadelphia in 1858, the Rev. Dudley Tyng (1825-1858) was the recognized leader. But, while standing by a piece of farm machinery on his place, the sleeve of his coat became entangled in the gears. His arm was pulled into the machinery and torn off. He died soon after. In the prime of life, Rev. Tyng was taken away from the direction of that great revival movement. His dying message to his associates in the work: "Stand up for Jesus," supplied the theme for this hymn. It was written by Rev. George Duffield, and was read at the close of a sermon he delivered on the Sunday following his friend's death.[4]

Onward, Christian Soldiers seems to fully embody the theme of the Church Militant given by Christ and Paul. Author, Sabine Baring-Gould (1834-1924), gave the background: "Whit-Monday [first Monday after Pentecost] is a great day for school festivals in Yorkshire. One Whit-Monday thirty years ago, it was arranged that our school should join forces with that of a neighboring village. I wanted the children to sing when marching from one village to another, but couldn't think of anything quite suitable; so I sat up at night, resolved that I would write something myself. "Onward, Christian Soldiers" was the result. It was written in great haste, and I am afraid some of the rhymes are faulty. Certainly, nothing has surprised me more than its popularity. I don't remember how it got printed first, but I know that very soon it found its way into several collections. I have written a few other hymns since then, but only two or three have become well-known."

This hymn was played in 1941 for American President, Franklin Roosevelt, at the request of the British leader, Winston Churchill, when the two met on board the HMS Prince of Wales to create the Atlantic Charter. In the 1939 film, *Stanley and Livingstone*, there is a scene where Dr. Livingstone leads African natives in singing the hymn. It was also sung at the end of the 1942 Academy Award winning movie *Mrs. Mini-*

ver, and at the funeral of President Dwight Eisenhower at the National Cathedral in Washington D.C., March 1969.[5]

The concept of a militant gospel by a militant church on a militant mission is largely unrecognized today. Instead, "me" focused doctrines dominate a feelings-based theology, concerning a feminine, non-judgmental God who always wants us to have the best opinion of ourselves. Reverent worship of a thrice holy Deity and enthusiastic obedience to His will and His work are all but abandoned. The modern American church forgets Christ is a King – a King who will return at the head of a white robed army, riding a white steed, slaying all resistance on planet earth. Yes, our Savior, the Lamb slain from the foundation of the world, is also a warrior. And when He sets up his throne in Jerusalem, He will rule the world with a rod of iron. We in America could go a long way in staunching the current apostasy by returning to the militant, orthodox theology seen in the old hymns, integral to our past greatness.

When Jesus cast out the moneychangers in the temple, found in John 2 and Matthew 21, quoting the Old Testament prophet, He declared: "It is written, 'My house shall be called a house of prayer;' but you are making it a robber's den" (Matthew 21:13). Not only do we need a rehearing of the command to the church universal, but we need a reminder of what is to be the activity of the local church. Jesus called His house a "house of prayer," indicating both an attitude and an activity. There should be a reverence for the physical building as well as the spiritual building. In the church today, you can find a variety of programs, and it is wonderful when a local body can meet the different needs of its people and community.

However, the basic ministries of the local church, which are worship, evangelism, education, and fellowship seen in Acts 2, are not to be neglected. Included in the heading of *worship*, and foundational to the work, is the discipline of prayer. Jesus did not call the temple a house of evangelism, or education, or fellowship, or preaching, though we are to do all those things. Quoting Isaiah 56:7, He called it a *house of prayer!*

I have found that the church talks a lot about prayer, but prays very little either corporately or individually. Usually, prayer is a formality in public and a last resort in private. Yet, Paul told the Thessalonians they were to "pray without ceasing" (1st Thessalonians 5:22). And James tells us "the effective prayer of a righteous man can accomplish much" (James 5:16). But it seems we don't really believe that. The weapons of our warfare are spiritual. Prayer is the most powerful spiritual weapon we have, next to God's Word, but we don't employ it – much to Satan's glee. Volumes have been written on prayer, and the bible is full of praying men and women and answers to their prayers, yet we do not follow their example. In scripture, prayer is often coupled with fasting, and we sure don't follow that one!

One story of prayer that always impressed me was that of the prophet Daniel, found in Daniel 10, mentioned earlier in chapter 4. There the prophet is seen praying and fasting for three weeks before the messenger of the Lord is able to break through Satanic resistance to answer him. From Daniel's encounter with the messenger angel, we get insight into spiritual warfare in the political realm. The angel of the prince of Persia fought God's emissary dispatched to the prophet from the very beginning of his prayer. Not until Michael the Archangel came to help could the original messenger get through. Upon delivering the answer to Daniel's supplication, the angel stated he had to return to battle the prince of Persia because the prince of Greece was on his way.

Daniel's inquiry before the Lord concerned the state of his people Israel, regarding their present captivity and their future survival. A sweeping revelation of coming gentile empires was given to the prophet in a near/far, or dual prophecy. The message to Daniel takes God's prophetic plan all the way to the end of the age in which we live. Through earnest prayer, the course of world politics was revealed to God's man nearly six hundred years before Christ. That truth has been recorded for us and kept through the centuries so that we could be informed about God's plan for His people and the future. Knowing the Lord's will and His revealed plans, we should pray to those ends. And as we see the day approaching and darkness descending, urgency of the church in prayer should be all the greater. Yet, there seems to be little urgency as America continues to fall.

When Israel faced national crisis, the prophets called the people to a Solemn Assembly. Joel 1:13-15:

> **13** Gird yourselves with sackcloth
> And lament, O priests;
> Wail, O ministers of the altar!
> Come spend the night in sackcloth
> O ministers of my God,
> For the grain offering and the drink offering
> Are withheld from the house of your God

14 Consecrate a fast,
Proclaim a solemn assembly;
Gather the elders
And all the inhabitants of the land
To the house of the Lord your God,
And cry out to the Lord.
15 Alas for the day!
For the day of the Lord is near,
And it will come as destruction from the Almighty.

Joel 2:15-17:

15 Blow a trumpet in Zion,
Consecrate a fast, proclaim a solemn assembly,
16 Gather the people, sanctify the congregation,
Assemble the elders,
Gather the children and the nursing infants.
Let the bridegroom come out of his room
And the bride out of her bridal chamber.
17 Let the priests, the Lord's ministers,
Weep between the porch and the altar,
And let them say, "Spare your people, O Lord,
And do not make your inheritance a reproach,
A byword among the nations.
Why should they among the peoples say,
'Where is their God?'"

When was the last time your church called you to a *solemn assembly* in order to avert God's wrath and seek His blessing?

This is one of those little known, unused spiritual weapons of our warfare.

I was recently given a book written by Dr. Chuck Lawless, professor of evangelism and missions at Southeastern Seminary, titled *The Potential and Power of Prayer – How to Unleash the Praying Church.* This pithy little volume makes some direct observations about what a real praying church actually looks like:

> "Most churches talk about prayer. Churches with prayer in their DNA actually *pray.* Churches that *talk* about prayer schedule prayer meetings (which relatively few members attend). Churches with prayer in their DNA *pray* at their prayer meetings. Churches that *talk* about prayer *hope* God will do great things. Churches that talk about prayer do *not* threaten the enemy. Churches with prayer in their DNA make the devil shake." [6]

Given the unprecedented Satanic activity on our planet right now, it doesn't appear we are causing much shaking in the devil's camp. We aren't even inhibiting his work, much less storming the gates of hell! Time to call the solemn assembly again. Time to pray and fast like Daniel, to cast off our self-sufficiency, to humble ourselves before a holy God and to seek His face like Solomon (2nd Chronicles 7:14). Then He will hear our prayer and forgive our sin and heal our land.

In order for the nation to get right, the church must get right. Just a few righteous can have a dynamic impact upon the direction of a country. Knowing this, the satanically controlled media works overtime in silencing and censoring the voice of Christians. As Rev. Tyng ordered upon his deathbed during the Philadelphia revival, "Stand up for Jesus!", we must no longer be silent in the face of overt satanic attack. God sought men to stand in the gap for Him during Judah's apostasy, and found none (Ezekiel 22:30). The gap is a break in a wall or battle line made by the enemy. If the gap is not closed, the enemy will widen it and pour through. Right now, it seems the whole wall is collapsing as the church looks on complacently rather than rushing into the breach to halt the devil's advance.

It might just take prayer and fasting... It might just take bible study and fellowship... It might just take church attendance and service... It might just take witnessing and evangelism... It might just take giving and sacrifice... But it also might take a phone call, a letter, an email, or a visit to a congressman. It might take standing in front of an abortion clinic, even if the FBI does threaten you! It might even take Christians running for public office from the lowest local to the highest federal. It's past time for Christians to get engaged again like the Founders were, for since the church handed the reigns of power over to the secularists, who passed them to the Marxists, America has spiraled downward.

It may not be too late to stop the nosedive, if the church can get it right with the Lord once again. It only takes a few in just the right place like Daniel and his three friends, or like Queen Esther who was placed by God at a critical juncture "for such a time as this" (Esther 4:14), in a critical place, to prevent the annihilation of the Jews. As Mordecai and Esther were the chosen servants of the hour, so are we. Our existence on this planet, on this continent, in this country, in this culture, and at this time, is no accident. Randomness, coincidence, luck, and happenstance do not exist for the Christian. "The steps of a good man are ordered of the Lord" (Psalm 37:23). We are called to a purpose. Our purpose is to glorify God in everything (1st Corinthians 10:31). We glorify Him in word and deed. We glorify Him in love and service. And we glorify Him in faith and obedience. Of course, when we fail in any of these, the opposite becomes true – we degrade His name and start down the road of apostasy.

When the early spiritual leaders of America saw the church begin to grow cold, they sought the face of God and called the people to repentance. Where is that much needed call today? Where is the weeping, and sackcloth, and mourning over sin? Where is the repentance, i.e., change of direction? Where is the needed revival and spiritual awakening that saved America of yesteryear?

We are, as of this writing, hot into the election season. Sadly, I see Christians and conservatives pinning all their hope, regarding our future, on one man. Unfortunately, that man is not Jesus Christ, our only hope!

In my own estimation, there may not be another election in the U.S. Why would I say such a thing? Because the church has allowed the wicked to take power. Now that they have it, it will be very difficult to get it back. Do not be surprised if the chosen conservative candidate for the American presidency is taken out in some fashion, or some black swan event occurs, or is staged, that will be an excuse not to hold elections, or postpone the installment of the next administration. The last four years ought to be proof enough that the wicked in power are not above doing what most citizens would consider unthinkable. Like Pollyanna, folks do not believe the forces at work are as nefarious as they are. Some of this naivete is genuine, but much of it is intentional as people refuse to exert the effort to do what is necessary to eradicate evil. It's always easier and more comfortable to do nothing. So, complacency, apathy, and non-commitment rule the day. I have an acronym for this problem: ALNC – pronounced *alnac*, meaning, apathy, lethargy, and non-commitment, a disease that infects us today. This is the real world-wide pandemic for which there is only one cure – salvation in Christ and obedience to His Word!

I have been hearing about little pockets of revival happening on some college campuses; small spiritual awakenings here and there. Of course, you hear very little about it in the mainstream media, for the "prince of the power of the air" (Ephesians 2:2) will have his way. Is it any wonder social media is so worldly and wicked? This exposes another phenomenon of recent years that is proving more harmful to human health, physically, emotionally, and spiritually than any other addiction known to man. Want to help move our population back to faith? Move them away from cell phones and electronic media. Studies now available prove conclusively the detrimental effect cell phones have upon your brain and your body, not to mention your mental and emotional health – our youth being particularly vulnerable. Some educators are finally waking up to the fact and prohibiting cell phone usage in school.

We've often speculated how antichrist would be able to

gain control over the world's population and economy. Microchip/cell phone technology, digital currency, and the World Economic Forum have provided the vehicle. Now, it's just a matter of forcing everyone to comply. The so-called COVID pandemic proved just how quickly it can and will be done. It showed us how a world population devoid of the truth of Christ will easily fall to the deception of Satan. It demonstrated how a general lack of Holy Spirit discernment left mankind wide open to the dictates of a wicked class whose goal is power. That goal remains as they gear up for the next crisis (pandemic?) that removes more freedom from the globe they seek to control, under the auspices of their father the devil. The apostle James tells us: "Submit therefore to God. Resist the devil and he will flee from you" (James 4:7). Our mission as the army of Christ is to resist the devil and his demons. It is to fight the good fight of faith, to get into the fray and stop the satanic advance whenever and wherever we can. We are to be the salt and light, storming the gates of hell, bringing in the last sheaves of the harvest before the Lord's return.

If you are not a part of this divine army, I urge you to join now. If you are not on the Lord's side, by default, you are on the side of the enemy. If your eternity in heaven is not secure, I implore you to make it so. The Bible tells us that we can be certain of our salvation: "And the testimony is this, that God has given us eternal life, and this life is in His Son. He who has the Son has the life; he who does not have the Son of God does not have the life. These things I have written to you who believe in the name of the Son of God, so that you may KNOW that you have eternal life" (1st John 5:11-13).

In the last words of Christ, in the last verses of His last book, He gives an invitation: "The Spirit and the bride say, 'Come.' And let the one who hears say, 'Come.' And let the one who is thirsty come; let the one who wishes take the water of life without cost" (Revelation 22:17). And, likewise, as we come to the end of this book, let me invite you once again to make Jesus Christ Lord and Savior. The invitation may not come again.

Conclusion

As stated throughout this book, apostasy is a spiritual problem. A spiritual problem manifests itself in carnal ways. Without Jesus Christ and the Holy Spirit's divine influence, man has no choice but to default to his fallen Adamic nature. That nature will grow more and more apparent as we see the day approaching (2nd Timothy 3). The birth pangs, or signs, Jesus spoke of in Matthew 24 and Luke 21, indicating the time of the end, will become more intense, and more frequent – just like we are experiencing right now. Yet, even though we know what is to come and how the future ultimately turns out, we have a duty to occupy until He comes (Luke 19:13). A victorious army occupies the territory it has conquered. We are not to give place to the devil or cede territory back to him. Having done all, we are to stand! (Ephesians 6:13).

In the opening chapters, we saw that our godly forefathers knew what it meant to stand. They stood against the tyrants of Europe. They stood against the perils of the sea and the harsh environment of an unsettled, untamed North American continent. They braved sickness, depravation, and death, all for the promise of liberty and hope for a new life of freedom, faith, and prosperity. And by faith, they, like Abraham, saw the promise far off, and like Abraham, believed (Hebrew 11:8-13).

If we are to put the brakes on our current rate of decline and salvage what is left of our country, we must return to the God of our heritage. We must humble ourselves and pray, and seek His face and turn from OUR wicked ways. If we are listening to the Lord, we will follow His formula for spiritual awakening – "Who knows, God may turn and relent, and withdraw His burning anger so that we will not perish..." "He [might just] turn and relent and leave a blessing behind Him..." (Jonah 3:9; Joel 2:14).

Christians, God is waiting on us!
Blessings,
Rev. Todd R. Gould

Addendum

During the writing of the last paragraphs of this book, the presidential election of 2024 came and went. The euphoria of Donald Trump's landslide victory, and the retaking of both legislative houses, remains. But I must caution that we do not overestimate the win, or underestimate the enemy. And I implore the Christian church, that finally prayed and got out to vote (making the election too big to rig), not to return to complacency.

I recall how, after the 9/11 attack in 2001, church attendance spiked for exactly two weeks before everyone went back to "business as usual." I hope we won't be so foolish as to believe that the devil has quit just because of an election. I certainly hope that we don't sit back now, thinking President Trump will fix everything! Don't forget, America's spiritual apostasy has not yet been remedied. God's judgment has not yet been mitigated. In His mercy, our God has given us a hope – perhaps one last opportunity to get it right, spiritually. Will we see the opportunity for what it is, or will we squander it again?

As we approach inauguration day, Satan is doing all he can to derail the incoming administration. Being the spiteful, implacable foe that he is, he will never cease to steal, kill, and destroy. Though his defeat was made sure at Calvary,

Satan relentlessly carries out his vindictive assault on mankind, because he knows his time is short. Likewise, though the current democrat administration knows it has been roundly defeated, imitating its father the devil, it continues the spiteful destruction of our Republic. The will of the American people is no consideration to this seditious lot in its scorched earth politics.

We must ask the obvious: "How has anything that has been done by the Biden cabal since the election been helpful to America?" The answer is: "Nothing has been helpful; all has been harmful." What greater statements can be made regarding its disdain, indeed hatred, of our country than:

- Intentional, unnecessary widening of the Ukraine war, putting us on the brink of World War III
- The attempted sale of border wall materials for pennies on the dollar
- Pardoning his own criminal son, and family, and setting up "pre-pardons" (whoever heard of such a thing) for other government criminals
- Commuting the sentences of 37 federal death row murderers, removing justice for the grieving victim's families
- Equally as bad, transferring eleven September 11 terrorists to Oman where they will be welcomed as heroes, again compromising justice for the victim's families
- Making illegal border crossings easier through phone apps
- Protecting illegal criminal aliens

- Destroying documents of the January 6th Select Committee
- Banning all offshore drilling and restricting drilling permits on federal lands
- Allowing unidentified drones to fly in our airspace
- Attempting to pass a pork laden continuing resolution bill at the last minute
- Sentencing Donald Trump in a sham conspiracy days before his inauguration
- And last but not least, presenting the Presidential Medal of Freedom to George Soros, a sworn enemy of the Republic – just to name a few.

These are the activities of a spiritual enemy who can only be defeated by spiritual weapons.

**My attempt to finish this book and get it to the publishers kept getting waylaid by the rapid-fire events of the Trump presidency. All that is being accomplished will have an impact on what's been written here, but I must end sometime. There is, however, one last event upon which I am compelled to comment due to its pertinence. That, of course, was the atrocious *Prayer Service* at the National Cathedral on January 21st. Unfortunately, the service included very little prayer and a mind-numbing amount of ceremony. But the real tragedy occurred when Episcopal Bishop, Mariann Budde, chose to ignore the gospel and instead deliver a personal diatribe against the President and his policies. She exposed her disbelief in God's Word and disqualification for the office. She proved herself to be the epitome of apostasy and what is wrong with Christendom in the U.S. This was another squandered opportunity to bring spiritual truth to our world and a blessing to our new government instead of a curse. How many *real* pastors would have cherished the opportunity Budde had (myself included) and done the right thing for both the President and our country?

May the American church follow the command of Paul: "First of all, then, I urge that entreaties and prayers, petitions and thanksgiving, be made on behalf of all men, for kings and all who are in authority, so that we may lead a tranquil and quiet life in all goodness and dignity. This is good and acceptable in the sight of God our Savior" (1st Timothy 2:1-3).

May the Lord have mercy on the United States of America and once again "shed His grace on thee."

In Him,
TRG

Endnotes

CHAPTER 1

1. "First Charter of Virginia (1606)," *www.encyclopedia-virginia.org/entries/first-charter-of-virginia1606* (March 15, 2023).
2. Ken Curtis, "Christianity in Jamestown – Key Facts and Events," *www.christianity.com/church/church-history/timeline/1600-1700/christianity-in-jamestown-11630060.html* (March 15, 2023).
3. Ibid.
4. "John Winthrop Dreams of a City on a Hill, 1630," *The American Yawp Reader, www.americanyawp.co/reader/colliding-cultures/john-winthrop-dreams-of-a-city-on-a-hill-1630/* (March 15, 2023).
5. "The Great Awakening: Origin, Key Figures and Influence," *www.christianity.com/church/church-history/timeline/1701-1800/the -great-awakening-11630212.html* (March 31, 2023).

CHAPTER 4

1. Paul Harvey, 1965: "If I Were the Devil," *www.youtube.com/watch?v=QGrWvrGDOXg* (May 24, 2023).
2. Jonathan Cahn, "The Stunning Secret Behind The Shooting At The Christian School in Nashville," *www.youtube.com/watch?v=_TMhlqFrrA* (June 6, 2023).

CHAPTER 5

1. "Marxist-Leninist Atheism," *Wikipedia, www.en.wikipedia.org/wiki/Marxist-Leninist_atheism* (April 7, 2023).
2. Ibid.
3. Ibid.
4. Ibid.
5. "The Difference Between Marxism And Communism," *Examarly, www.blog.examarly.com/upsc/difference-between-marxism-and-communism/* (April 7, 2023)
6. "History of the Communist Party USA," *Wikipedia, www.en.wikipedia.org/wiki/History_of_the_Communist_Party_USA* (April 7, 2023).
7. Ibid.
8. "Barack Obama and the Communist Party," *KeyWiki, www.keywiki.org/Barack_Obama_and_the_Communist_Party* (April 7, 2023).
9. "During Cold War Top Intel Officers, FBI Chief Comey and CIA Top Spy Brennan, Voted for Communists," *Conservative Base, www.conservativebase.com/during-*

cold-war-top-intel-officers-fbi-chief-comey-andcia-top-spy-brennan-voted-for-communists/ (June 26, 2023).

10. "An Outburst of Awakening," *American Renewal Project, www.mail.google.com/mail/u/0/?ik=a8f6518d50&view=pt&search-all&permthid=thread-f:1767321037080138007&simpl=msg- f1767321037080138007* (May 30, 2023).

CHAPTER 9

1. "Ecclesia (Church)," *Simple English Wikipedia, the free encyclopedia, www.simple.wkipedia.org/wiki/Ecclesia_(Church)#:~:text=Latin ecclesia%2C from Greek ekklesia,"%2C or "convocation"* (April 18, 2024).
2. "Spiritual Warfare," *HymnTime.com, www.hymntime.com>tch>top>spiritualwarfare295hymns* (April 19, 2024).
3. "Battle Hymn of the Republic," *Kennedy-Center.org, www.kennedy-center.org/education/resouces-for-educators/classroom-resources/media-and-interactives/media/musicstory-behind-the-song/* (April 19, 2024).
4. "Stand Up, Stand Up for Jesus," *HymnTime.com, www.hymntime/tch/htm/s/t/a/n/standufj.htm* (April 19, 2024)
5. "Onward, Christian Soldiers (Baring-Gould)," *HymnTime.com, www.hymntime.com/tch/htm/o/n/w/a/onwardcs.htm* (April 19, 2024).
6. Chuck Lawless, *The Potential and Power of Prayer – How to Unleash the Praying Church* (Carol Stream: Tyndale Momentum, 2022), 9.

To reach Pastor Gould regarding interim work
or pulpit supply, contact:

IMI/SOS International
P.O. Box 116
Hudsonville, MI 49426
office@imisos.org
616.797.9990
Or: *pastorgould1953@gmail.com*

www.ingramcontent.com/pod-product-compliance
Lightning Source LLC
Chambersburg PA
CBHW020003290326
41935CB00007B/291

9780960011544